Twilight of the Evening Lands

TWILIGHT

OF THE

EVENING

LANDS

Oswald Spengler—
A Half Century Later

JOHN F. FENNELLY

THE BROOKDALE PRESS

NEW YORK

For information, address the publisher:
The Brookdale Press
60 East 42 Street, New York 10017

Standard Book Number: 0–912650–01–X
Library of Congress Catalog Number: 72–78519
Printed in the United States of America

Contents

42537

ACKNOWLEDGMENTS

I am indebted to numerous individuals who advised and assisted me in the preparation of this study. First I should mention Professor Manfred Schröter who introduced me to the Spengler Archive in Munich, and Dr. Anton Koktanek, the Director of the Archive. Next, I am deeply indebted to Mr. Peter Wolff for his editorial assistance in several revisions of the manuscript. Professor R. W. Lee of Princeton University provided many helpful criticisms and suggestions for my treatment of the arts. Dr. Wood B. Carper of the General Theological Seminary of New York furnished a number of constructive suggestions for the section on religion. Mr. Herbert Prochnow, retired president of the First National Bank of Chicago, performed a similar service for the section on economics, and Mr. Frederick Yeiser, retired music critic of the Cincinnati Enquirer, was very helpful in connection with my section on music. Finally, I am grateful to Alfred A. Knopf, Inc. for its generous permission to quote extensively from *The Decline of the West*, as well as from other works by Spengler published by this firm.

JOHN F. FENNELLY

Introduction

WE LIVE TODAY in an atmosphere of gloomy foreboding and of growing doubts as to the prospects for our western civilization. Perhaps the leading contributor to this prevailing mood has been the invention of the nuclear and thermonuclear weapons and the resulting threat of a global holocaust which hangs like the sword of Damocles over every nation of the world. Other contributing factors have been the emergence of the cold war and the deterioration of international relations, the decay of our cities, and the rise of racial and student unrest throughout the Free World accompanied by a startling increase in violence of all kinds. Finally, we have suddenly become aware of the serious threat to our environment caused largely by the advances in industrial technology and the rapid growth of population.

As a long time student of Oswald Spengler I have become convinced that his master work, *The Decline of the West* represents one of the best expressions of the spirit of our times. From this it follows that Spengler's theories of cultural growth and decay have a significant relevance for an understanding of our modern world and that a contemporary re-examination of his historical philosophy can throw much light on the dark and confused areas of our western civilization.

The first volume of Spengler's *Der Untergang des Abendlandes* (translated into English as *The Decline of the West,* but which means literally "The Going Under of the Evening Lands") was published in German[1] in 1918. The second volume appeared in 1922. An English edition of the first volume was published in the United States in 1926 and the second volume in English followed shortly in[2] 1928. A full half century, therefore, has elapsed since the initial appearance of this work in the original German, and more than forty years since it became available in English.

I first became aware of the *Decline* in 1928 while teaching economics and history at Columbia University. I can never forget the excitement I felt in ploughing through more than one thousand pages of fairly abstruse writing. It struck my consciousness with the impact of the burst of a hand grenade. With the naiveté of youth I swallowed the Spenglerian philosophy of history like a hungry trout, and my enthusiasm was fully equal to that of John Keats—"On First Looking into Chapman's Homer."

My deep interest in Spengler has served as a catalyst for a continuing adult education in philosophy and history. This study, covering a period of more than forty years, has altered substantially my original uncritical acceptance of Spengler's theories. Thus, I have become progressively more

---

[1]A second, and considerably modified, edition of the first volume appeared in 1922 and became the standard text of the work.
[2]Both volumes of the edition in English were published by Alfred A. Knopf, New York.

aware of the author's dogmatism, his many exaggerations and omissions, his repetitiveness, and his extreme efforts to force recalcitrant facts into a preconceived mould. Nevertheless, despite my awareness of such shortcomings, I have managed to retain much of my early enthusiasm for the brilliance of his historical imagination, and his innumerable fascinating insights into historical relationships. Although somewhat tarnished by the passage of the years, Spengler's image still displays for me a lustre that is almost unique in my intellectual experience.

The rapid unfolding of events in recent years has convinced me that the time is ripe for a fresh examination of Spengler's philosophy of history, despite the thousands of pages that have been written on this subject.[3] The present study, however, attempts to avoid the danger of becoming just one more critique of Spengler's philosophy and methodology, since this approach has been followed almost ad nauseum by an army of professional critics. Instead, the primary emphasis herein lies in an examination of the author's various predictions as to a decline of western civilization, and of their relevance for the modern world after the passage of a half century. Thus, the study seeks to determine the extent to which the events since the end of World War I tend to support or refute the author's predictions of decline. As one contemporary writer has observed:—

"The most important confirmation of any theory is in its predictions. This, then, leads to the question of our position

---

[3]*Der Streit um Spengler* by Manfred Schröter, published in 1922, lists over 400 different commentaries on the *Decline* in the form of books, essays, reviews and editorials that appeared in print during the four years that followed the initial appearance of the first volume in 1918.

3

in history. Like it or not, make any objections you please against Spengler's intuitive approach and "unscientific" ways, his questionable conceptualizations, his metaphysics, dogmatism and militaristic spirit; the fact remains that his predictions made fifty years ago and long before atomic war, the emergence of the U.S.S.R. and China were even dreamt of, proved to be alarmingly correct, being verified to an extent far surpassing the success of many neat little mathematical models in vogue in modern sociology. . . . The *Decline of the West* is not a hypothesis or prophecy; it is an accomplished fact."[4]

Moreover, this study is not directed to the scholarly world, although I am confident that the scholarship in these pages will stand up under critical scrutiny. The audience I am attempting to reach is that of the average college under-graduate and that of the intelligent adult layman. For these classes of readers it seems correct to assume that only a small percentage has an intimate familiarity with the philosophy of the *Decline*. Although a progressive revival of interest in Spengler has taken place since World War II such interest is still limited largely to professional scholars and advanced students of history.

In order to appeal to a broader spectrum of readers I have deemed it advisable to devote the first three chapters of the study to a presentation of the story of *The Decline of the West*. Chapter I is a brief biographical sketch of the author; Chapter II offers a simplified explanation of Spengler's Theories; Chapter III sets forth the principal criticisms

---

[4]George Braziller, Inc. from *Robots, Men and Minds* by Ludwig von Bertalanffy reprinted with the permission of the publisher. Copyright (c) 1967 Ludwig von Bertalanffy.

raised against Spengler's philosophy of history, and a brief discussion of his successors in the writing of cyclical history. Chapter IV attempts to come to grips with the heart of the problem—The relevance for the contemporary world of Spengler's predictions of a decline of our western civilization.

Very early in my graduate studies I became convinced that all historical interpretation is subjective to a greater or lesser degree. It is almost impossible for an historian to write of events, either of the remote past or of the present, without having the narrative colored by his own personality and temperament. Certainly this was true of Oswald Spengler, and equally true of his many critics. In his more humble moments Spengler admitted that the vast panorama of history which he painted was true for him, and not necessarily so for others.

Moreover, despite his vast erudition, Spengler must be classified essentially as an amateur historian. He had none of the rigorous training in the sifting of data on which the positivist or "scientific" school of historians prides itself. This very lack, however, was undoubtedly responsible for permitting free sway for Spengler's extraordinary historical imagination.

If Spengler is to be considered an amateur, a commentator like myself should have no illusions as to his own limitations. Despite a brief training in the methods of a professional historian, and a much more extensive training as a professional economist, I cannot consider myself an expert. To qualify as such in all the areas covered by the *Decline* would require several lifetimes of intensive study. In the words which Tennyson placed in the mouth of the aged

Ulysses: "Life piled on life were all to little, and of one to me little remains." The conclusions set forth in this study, therefore, will not only be colored by my own personality but will also be those of an amateur.

No attempt is made herein to suggest national policies that might avert the dangers that now threaten our society. Instead, my primary purpose has been to make the reader fully aware of these dangers in the hope that there still may be time to change the direction in which the western world seems to be moving. Moreover, for many of us who grew up to believe in a progressive amelioration of human society, almost as a religious faith, acceptance of a philosophy of impending doom may result in outright despair. Perhaps a thorough digestion of Spengler's theories can lead to a middle ground between unlimited optimism and unbridled pessimism—a philosophy of life based upon certain hard realities of existence, and a realization that there still remain open many avenues for constructive and satisfactory activities in this world of today.

I am encouraged to this task by the monumental failure of Spengler's professional critics. If ever a piece of work could be buried under an avalanche of criticism *The Decline of the West* would have disappeared forever forty five years ago. Nevertheless, it has refused to die, and today is demonstrating a vitality which must astound the remnant of those critics that has been able to survive the intervening years. It is a common truism that present day academicians tend to know more and more about less and less, and that very few of them are able to see over the barriers separating their own narrow specialties from other fields of learning.

Introduction

Perhaps the time has come for an amateur whose view of the whole forest is not obscured by the blank wall of trees surrounding any particular camp site.

J.F.F.

1

The Man

OSWALD SPENGLER was born in 1880 in the town of Blankenburg in the Harz Mountains in northern Germany in a middle class family of moderate means.[1] His father, Bernhard Spengler came from a long line of mining technicians who, several generations earlier, had moved from southern Germany to the mining area in the Harz Mountains. Probably because of the relative exhaustion of these mines, Bernhard Spengler elected not to follow the family profession but became instead a minor official in the Imperial German postal service. Oswald's mother, Pauline Spengler, was born Pauline Grantzow. Her parents were both professional ballet dancers, the father being ballet master and her mother ballet mistress in Berlin. One of Pauline's sisters, Adele,

---

[1]Most of the material in this biographical summary has been gleaned from the comprehensive biography, "Oswald Spengler in Seiner Zeit" by Anton M. Koktanek, published in Munich in 1968.

achieved considerable fame as a ballerina in Paris and in Moscow. When she died in 1876, Adele left an inheritance of 120,000 marks to Oswald's mother, a sum which in those days represented a moderate fortune.

Oswald was the oldest of four children. His three sisters, Adele, Gertrud, and Hildegard, were all born between 1881 and 1885. Adele, apparently Oswald's favorite sister, had exceptional talents as a painter and as a musician. She suffered, however, from a high degree of emotional instability and finally committed suicide in 1917. Hildegard, the youngest, was married in 1908 to Fritz Kornhardt who was killed in action at Verdun in 1917. Sometime after the end of the war, Hildegard moved to Munich to live with her brother. Her diary, kept faithfully from childhood until her death in 1942, has become one of the chief sources of information on Spengler's life.

The Spengler home was far from a happy one. The parents had little or no love for one another. The father took pride in being a government official but apparently was not interested in anything else. The mother, perhaps frustrated because her dumpy figure prevented her from being a ballet dancer, became something of a petty tyrant with her children. She spent most of her waking hours with her painting and music. Later in life Spengler wrote that there had been no books in the family home; that his mother read only the newspaper and his father read nothing.

Young Oswald was a fragile sickly child and even at an early age suffered from migraine headaches which were to torment him throughout his whole life. He also had a well developed anxiety complex about almost everything. He was much given to daydreaming, his phantasies usually taking the form of leading German armies to victory throughout the world.

Koktanek, in his biography, discusses these phantasies in great detail and clearly regards them as something sinister and as a portent of the mature Spenglerian philosophy. Such emphasis seems unjustified. Many boys, particularly those of introspective tendencies, go through a daydreaming phase, and it is generally considered a normal aspect of boyhood.

It should also be remembered that the years of Spengler's boyhood were those of the German Empire's greatest glory. The coming of the railroad had revolutionized life in Central Europe and made possible the creation of modern Germany. Victorious in two wars, the German Empire, during the last two decades of the 19th Century, was threatening the industrial leadership of Britain and the scientific and cultural leadership of both France and Britain. At that time Germany had become a mecca for American scholars who flocked in large numbers to German universities to do graduate work in a wide variety of fields. Small wonder then that a German boy growing up in this heady atmosphere should reflect in his daydreams a pride in this mighty upsurge of national achievement.

In his capacity as a postal official Bernhard Spengler was forced to move his family on several occasions during Oswald's boyhood. The final move took place in 1890 when the family settled in the City of Halle. Here, in this university town, the Spengler children received their secondary school education. Oswald had a thorough grounding in Latin and Greek and in mathematics which were to become his special fields of study. With his withdrawn personality and frail physique he was not a ready mixer with other children. Except for his sisters, he was particularly unhappy in the presence of girls, a characteristic that stayed with him throughout his life. Thus, at an early age, he was clearly marked for a scholarly or monkish existence.

Spengler also showed a strong predilection for poetry and drama during his secondary school years and tried his youthful hand at writing both. His love of poetry and music was an important factor throughout his career and shines out clearly in the pages of the *Decline*. It was at this time that he developed his great enthusiasm for Goethe and Nietzsche who were to be the most important intellectual influences in his life. In the case of Nietzsche it was probably the poetic aspect of the latter's writings that appealed to him as much as the actual philosophic content. Perhaps under the influence of Nietzsche the youthful Spengler developed also a strong aversion to orthodox Christianity and the Church.

Spengler graduated from high school in 1899 but did not proceed at once to a university, perhaps as a result of the final lingering illness of his father. Death finally came to the father in 1901 and Oswald entered upon his university career in the fall of that year. Since his father left nothing to his family but his blessings, Spengler's university education was made possible solely by the legacy which his mother had received from her sister Adele. Shortly after the father's death the mother insisted on moving the family back to their former home in Blankenburg. Here she remained until her death in 1910.

As was a German custom at the time, Spengler elected to

spend one year each at three different universities. First he attended the University of Munich; he then proceeded to the University of Berlin; and spent his final year at the University of Halle. At all three institutions he continued his studies of Greece and Rome, mathematics and the physical sciences. In Munich he was also absorbed by the music which that city offered, and in Berlin by a study of the drama.

In his final year at Halle he prepared for his doctoral degree by writing a dissertation on Heraclitus, the pre-Socratic philosopher who lived about 550–475 B.C. Spengler's dissertation was a competent, if not particularly distinguished piece of work. It is easy to understand why Heraclitus, known as the "Dark Philosopher," and whose writings exist today only in fragmentary form, should have appealed to Spengler. He was an aristocrat and was exiled from Athens as a result of the democratic upheavals of the time. In his lonely existence he developed a profound system of metaphysics based upon the fundamental unity of all nature. Taking fire as the primary substance, he held that in nature the sole actuality is change. The rhythm of events and order in change is the reason or *logos* of the universe. One phrase by Heraclitus, which struck a sympathetic response in Spengler was "War is the creator of all things."

Spengler presented his dissertation and appeared for his final examination in the fall of 1903. On this attempt he was turned down because, in the opinion of his examiners, he had cited insufficient references. (This was a general characteristic of practically all of Spengler's later writings.) In the spring of 1904 he made a second try at the final examination and was finally passed. In order to qualify fully as a high school teacher it was then necessary for Spengler to present a secondary dissertation. This study bore the title of "The Development of the Organ of Sight in the Higher Ranks of the Animal Kingdom." It was presented to the State Board of Examiners and approved.

Although now qualified to start on a teaching career, Spengler was required to spend two years on trial as a teacher. First he taught at a school in Saarbrücken, in what was known as his seminar year—probably as an assistant teacher. He then moved to a school in Düsseldorf to undergo a year of testing. Having successfully surmounted these hurdles, he obtained an assignment as a full-fledged high school teacher at a Gymnasium in Hamburg. He started his work in Hamburg in January 1908 as a teacher of mathematics and the physical sciences, and added thereto the teaching of history and German literature.

Apparently Spengler was an able and very successful teacher. Many years later one of his students at Hamburg wrote a moving tribute to the inspirational qualities of his teaching, and to his ability to maintain strict discipline in his classes merely through the strength and dignity of his personality.

Unfortunately the cold climate of Hamburg was not suitable for his frail physique. During the Hamburg years he suffered constantly from terrible attacks of migraine headaches. Some of these were so intense that he went through brief periods of amnesia, when he could not remember where he was, or even his own name.

In photographs taken during the first decade of the present century, Oswald Spengler appears as a strikingly handsome young man. With thick dark hair, he wore a full beard pointed at the end in the Empire fashion of the day. He always dressed in formal attire with high wing collars and wide cravats. During the second decade of the century he rapidly succumbed to baldness and removed first his beard and then his mustache. In his later years Spengler's most outstanding physical characteristic was his massive head surmounted by the huge bald dome of his forehead. A sculptured bust done in 1928 shows vividly this huge forehead, with its heavy eyebrows and the almost terrifying forcefulness of the face beneath.

Spengler's mother died suddenly in February 1910 and left Oswald an inheritance that gave him a moderate degree of financial independence. He stayed at his position in Hamburg for another year but then decided to leave teaching and try his hand as an independent writer. He moved to Munich in 1911 in the hope of finding in southern Germany a climate more suitable for his health. He took living quarters in the vicinity of the university and lived in that area for the rest of his life.

When he first settled in Munich, Spengler had not yet decided to which field of writing he would dedicate his talents. At the outset he dabbled briefly with poetry and drama and wrote one short story that was more sentimental than distinguished. Shortly, however, he found himself turning to the fields of politics and history. Although he had long cherished the idea of writing a book of political observations he was driven strongly in this direction by the international events which were rapidly unfolding in Europe—the growing armaments race, the increasing polarity in the alignment of the central European powers against the Entente of

France, Britain and Russia, and the successions of international crises. When the Agadir crisis occurred in 1911 Spengler suddenly became convinced that all of Europe was marching down the road toward an inevitable global conflict which would mark the beginning of the end of European culture. He also believed that Germany was being led to destruction by the stupidity of its leadership in permitting the nation to be encircled by an alignment of unfriendly powers.

The book, which was originally to have been called "Conservative and Liberal," soon took off on its own. As the study progressed, the scope of the work steadily widened and deepened. It finally emerged as a comparative study of eight high Cultures of the human race; delineating for each its birth, growth, decline and death. A secondary motif (perhaps even the primary purpose) of the study was its emphasis upon events of the 19th and 20th centuries, demonstrating, according to the author, the beginning of the period of decline of the Culture of Western Europe. Finally, by comparing the course of developments in the other High Cultures, Spengler professed an ability to foretell the unfolding of future events in our own Western Culture. By the outbreak of the war the organization of the work had taken final form and the first draft had been completed.

Such briefly was the origin and development of Spengler's master work—*The Decline of the West*. It should be emphasized here that this study was not a product of the events of the war. Instead, the approach of the war had served merely as a catalyst for the development of the author's ideas. Also it should be pointed out that it was purely fortuitous that the publication of the first volume of the *Decline* in the summer of 1918 coincided with the collapse of Germany.

Spengler suffered severely during the war years. The legacy left by his mother was invested chiefly in foreign securities, the income from which disappeared automatically with the outbreak of war. As a result, he was forced to live under conditions of extreme poverty, with scarcely enough to eat, practically no heat in his living quarters and working mainly by candle light. He also suffered constantly from severe headaches. On at least two occasions he was called up for military service, but each time was rejected because of a weak heart and faulty vision. A photograph of Spengler taken in 1917 shows vividly, in the gaunt harassed countenance, what he had endured.

Despite the handicaps and privations, Spengler struggled on with his labors throughout the war years. Working in almost complete isolation, and without the background of training as a professional historian, he lacked the benefit of friendly advice and criticism. Such shortcomings undoubtedly help to account for the many errors that appeared in the first edition.

Around the end of 1917 or early in 1918 the first volume was ready for publication, but Spengler experienced considerable difficulty in finding a publisher. After some abortive attempts he finally succeeded in having the book published in Vienna. After a brief interlude, the *Decline* began to achieve a wide-spread popularity which grew steadily during the next few years. By 1919 the name of the previously unknown author, without professional standing, had become a household word throughout the German speaking world. By 1922, when the second volume appeared, more than 100,000 copies of the first volume had been sold, a tremendous circulation for such a ponderous, obscure work.

After the unexpected collapse of their military power in 1918, and the subsequent internal chaos culminating in the disastrous inflation of 1923, the German people were ready for a prophet of doom. They found many parallels between the disasters of their own country and a general decline of western civilization.

While the *Decline* achieved an immense popularity with the general public it was greeted by widespread condemnation on the part of the professionals. Historians, archeologists, art critics, theologians, anti-German intellectuals, etc. all joined in an attack that was almost overwhelming. Since these criticisms are treated in some detail in a subsequent chapter, it will suffice at this point to observe that prior to 1925 the only two voices of any professional standing that rallied to Spengler's defense were those of Professor Manfred Schröter of Munich and Eduard Meyer, the distinguished German scholar of ancient history. It should be noted also that this flood of criticism had the effect of causing Spengler to publish a revised and considerably modified second edition of the first volume in 1922.

The appearance of the second volume, also in 1922, did little to enhance Spengler's reputation amongst the professionals. They found in it merely an expansion of the theme of the first volume, with the same dogmatism and the same repetitiveness. Although we shall return to this subject a little later, it is clear that by 1924 Spengler's popularity in Germany had passed its peak and was rapidly fading. With the stabilization of the currency in 1925 and the beginning of a new period of prosperity the German public turned its attention away from gloomy prophecies to the immediate realities of the present.

The flood of royalties that poured into Spengler's pocket after 1918 did have the effect of causing a vast improvement in the author's standard of living. He moved to a larger and more comfortable apartment, and his widowed sister Hildegard Kornhardt, with her daughter, came to live with him and served as his housekeeper and constant companion throughout the balance of his life. He was now able to travel as he wished. He journeyed extensively in Germany delivering speeches and lectures, made many visits to his beloved Italy, one to Spain, and one to the Baltic countries of Lithuania, Latvia and Finland. He also attempted to make a trip to Russia, but was unsuccessful in his efforts to obtain a Russian visa.

When we come to a consideration of Spengler's postwar political activities it must be admitted candidly that he made something of a fool of himself. It was the old story of the philosopher turned statesman, a mistake made by Plato[2] at Syracuse, but one which Goethe scrupulously avoided in his ministerial duties for the tiny Duchy of Weimar. Nevertheless, it is not difficult to understand the forces that led Spengler into political activity. During the first five years

---

[2]Arnold Toynbee has described Plato's political activities in the following words: "Plato longed to translate his vision into real life, and naively hoped to find a short cut to this remote goal by persuading the contemporary despot of Syracuse, Dionysius II, to depose himself by imposing Plato's constitutional blueprint on his subjects. In his political ideas and activities, Plato was a child of his age. The Plato who towers above time and place is Plato the poet and the seer." *Hellenism,* by Arnold J. Toynbee, Oxford University Press, New York and London, 1959, p. 131.

To a certain degree the same words may be applied to Oswald Spengler.

after the end of the war the German people went through an agony of turmoil bordering on chaos that few foreigners have troubled to comprehend:—the Bolshevist oriented Sparticide revolts in the cities, the rise of Fascism at the other extreme under the leadership of Hitler, the occupation of the Ruhr by French and Belgian troops, and finally the culminating disaster of the great inflation that left the population largely bankrupt.

Oswald Spengler was the philosopher and prophet of the day and he was urged on all sides to play an active role in politics. For his own part he was ready for the role. As an ultra-conservative he had no faith in democracy in general, and none in the Weimar Republic in particular. In what he saw as an approaching age of dictatorships and Caesarism, Spengler believed sincerely that the only hope for restoring Germany to a position in the front ranks of the Western World was through the leadership of a strong dictator. Nor was he alone in this view. It was shared by many leading industrialists, by most of the military leaders, and by a scattering of intellectuals. These people had grown up in an atmosphere of order and of obedience to the State, and they were miserable in the presence of the disorders they saw all around them.

It is to Spengler's great credit that he steadfastly refused to become a member of the Nazi party. There was enough in common between the Spenglerian philosophy and the professed ideals of Hitler to give plausability to the idea of such a union. In fact, the Nazis attempted to present Spengler and Nietzsche as their spiritual fathers. There was more justification for this in the case of Spengler than in the case of Nietzsche, because the latter had displayed a strong anti-

19

pathy for the German people and an even stronger repugnance for the spirit of German nationalism.

Spengler was approached repeatedly by Gregor Strasser, one of the more liberal intellectuals of the early Nazi leaders. The latter urged him to become the leading propagandist for the cause. This role was rejected by Spengler. He was repelled by the fanatical anti-semitism of Hitler, by the violence and brutality of Hitler's followers, and by the general tawdriness of the whole movement. Apropos of Hitler, Spengler once declared that what the country needed was a hero, and not an heroic tenor.

Spengler's first venture into political writing was a little book published in 1919 with the title "Prussianism and Socialism."[3] In it he advocated for Germany a corporative society in which all the different economic elements would be united under the leadership of a strong but benevolent dictator. Spengler contrasted the British ideal of freedom with that of the German. The British ideal, he asserted, was freedom to make money under a fairly loose supervision by the government. The Prussian ideal, on the other hand, was a kind of socialism which restricted the money-making freedom of the individual for the benefit of the whole, but gave him freedom to rise to any position in the hierarchy which his abilities merited.

There was nothing novel in this Spenglerian thesis. As critics pointed out, it was largely a repetition of doctrines enunciated earlier by such social philosophers as Pareto.

---

[3]*Preussentum und Sozialismus* was published by the Munich firm of Beck. Under the influence of August Albers, Spengler's friend and admirer, and a manuscript reader for Beck, all of Spengler's subsequent works were handled by this firm.

The book was received with little enthusiasm in Germany and did nothing to enhance Spengler's reputation as a thinker.

Then followed a series of speeches and lectures in the same general tenor, but only a few of these were ever published. Spengler also engaged in discussions with a group of German industrialists, of which the leader was his friend, Paul Reusch. Their objective was to find the right individual to lead in the overthrow of the Weimar Republic and assume the role of dictator. Their choice finally centered on General von Seeckt who at that time was head of the small German army permitted by the terms of the Versailles Treaty. Spengler had already become convinced of the omnipotence of the press in the modern world and his work in this movement was largely devoted to an effort to find means of uniting the German press in support of the objective. In this he failed completely. General von Seeckt refused to be a party to the undertaking and the whole plan died aborning.

By 1925, with the stabilization of the German currency and the economy, Spengler faded out of the political scene. He had gradually been forced to realize that political activity was not his forte. He wrote and spoke above the heads of his audiences, while the working classes looked askance at his old-fashioned aristocratic ideas. As a result, he turned his attention once more to the fields of metaphysics and history.

In the preface to the second volume of the *Decline* Spengler had announced his intention of writing a major work of metaphysics. Later, on many occasions, in letters and conversations, he referred to the important metaphysical work on which he was engaged. Nothing of this kind appeared in print during his lifetime, and it was not until a full generation after his death that the fruit of his labor was published in a book entitled *Urfragen—Fundamental Questions.*

During the same period Spengler engaged himself in another endeavor. Some years after the publication of the *Decline* he became convinced, chiefly under the influence of Leo Frobenius, a German anthropologist, that he had left an important gap in his study of history. In his master work Spengler had maintained that prior to the birth of a culture, primitive man was historyless, and, after the death of the culture, returned to a state of non-history. He realized belatedly that the problem could not be disposed of in such a summary fashion, and that primitive men had histories of real importance for the modern student. Spengler plunged into this study of pre-history with his accustomed vigor and enthusiasm. Some fragments of this work were published in 1952 by Spengler's niece, Dr. Hildegard Kornhardt, in a compilation of his speeches and essays. A more complete compilation of this work in pre-history was published in 1966 under the title of *Frühzeit der Weltgeschichte— Early Period of World History.*

It seems desirable to consider these two apparently separate endeavors simultaneously because they became inextricably mingled in the writing. During the ten years prior to her death in 1959, Dr. Kornhardt labored incessantly, first, to decipher the thousands of almost illegible notes which Spengler had dashed off and tossed into a series of files, and, second, to arrange them in some kind of logical order. After Dr. Kornhardt's death a Spengler archive was established in the offices of the publisher Beck under the direction of Dr. Anton Koktanek. The latter continued the task of sorting and arranging and finally produced the two volumes mentioned above.

The great bulk of Spengler's notes were brief paragraphs written in the form of aphorisms. It seems evident that Spengler, in his metaphysical work, was attempting to follow the aphoristic style of Nietzsche. A limited number of the fragments were in the form of complete essays and clearly were planned as chapters for his book on pre-history.

It is not given to many men to write more than one great work, and Spengler certainly failed in his attempt to do so. True, he was handicapped by a mild stroke which he suffered in 1927, and from which he never fully recovered. Nevertheless, it appears very doubtful that, even in the absence of this illness, anything of real significance would have evolved from this work.

The book *Fundamental Questions,* published in the form of aphorisms, is baffling to a degree. The first section, entitled "The Flame," is largely a conglomeration of unconnected, semi-mystical pronouncements. The last section, "Man and Fate," is a rehash of the ideas already set forth in the *Decline.* In between are various sections in which metaphysical ideas are thrown together with the author's observations on pre-history.[4] One would like to believe that, had he lived, Spengler would never have permitted this volume to appear in print.

"Early Period of World History" is a much more orderly

---

[4]For further commentary on these two posthumously published books, the reader's attention is directed to the discussion of Spengler's metaphysics in Chapter III.

piece of work but is also without real significance. Spengler was neither an anthropologist nor a paleontologist and was ill-equipped for the task. His delineation of four stages in the development of man seems highly arbitrary and his treatment of such periods as that of the Achaean Greeks throws no new light on the subject.

Spengler did produce one monograph during his lifetime that was inspired by his study of pre-history. This little volume was published in 1931 in Germany with the title *Der Mensch und die Technik* and translated into English as *Man and Technics*. It was largely an expansion of the theme set forth in the chapter, "The Machine" in the second volume of the *Decline*. The author extended the story of technics backwards in time to the first appearance of the human hand[5] and its use as a weapon. It was extended forward in time by Spengler's prediction that the colored races, having adopted the complex technics of modern western civilization, would employ these methods in an effort to destroy the dominant white races.

Shortly before his death Spengler turned once more to the field of political writing. In 1933 he published a book entitled *Die Jahre der Entscheidung*; later published in English as *The Hour of Decision*. This book, although dealing largely with current events, was considerably more philosophical than his earlier political efforts, and closer in spirit

[5]In "Man and Technics" Spengler asserted a surprisingly naive theory of evolution. He believed that evolutionary changes in species developed suddenly as a kind of catastrophic event. He also stated his belief that the development of the human hand had occurred only a few thousand years before the beginning of recorded history which he placed around 3,000 B.C. Recent discoveries in Africa, however, provide convincing evidence that the development of the human hand had caused man's immediate predecessors to become wielders of weapons at least 800,000 years ago.

to the temper of the *Decline*. In it Spengler foretold the coming of a second world war and pointed out the dangerous position of Germany in this connection.

The main theme, however, lies in two lengthy chapters, entitled respectively "The White World Revolution," and "The Colored World Revolution." In the former Spengler describes the rise to power in the Western World of the labor unions and the resulting artificial or political wage levels of the workers involved. This situation in turn has caused the white entrepreneurs to establish factories in backward nations in order to take advantage of the much lower wage rates prevailing in such areas.

The resulting gift of advanced industrial techniques has enabled the colored races (among which he includes the Russian race) to mount a world revolution of their own. In Spengler's view, the white world is threatened by a class war within and a race war without, and his great fear was that these two forces may combine for a final overthrow of our civilization. The only possible salvation for the western world, in Spengler's opinion, can come from the development of a spirit of unity, discipline and self-sacrifice amongst the white peoples. Although he describes this as the "Prussian" spirit, Spengler is careful to point out that he does not mean the German people alone but merely the kind of spirit and discipline that made Prussia great.

Perhaps the most important aspect of *The Hour of Decision* is that it marked Spengler's complete break with the Nazis. His repudiation of Hitler and his followers, however, was so subtly phrased that the latter were not aware of the book's import until some time after its publication. Thus, he never mentions the name of Hitler. His only direct reference to the Nazi party is the following sentence; "And the National Socialists believe that they can afford to ignore the world or oppose it, and build their castles-in-the-air without creating a possibly silent, but very palpable reaction from abroad."[6]

Nevertheless, there are numerous indirect attacks on the Nazis which a careful reading of the book discloses. To show the flavor of these it must suffice here to cite only the following two:

"But in speaking of race, it is not intended in the sense in which it is the fashion among anti-semites in Europe and America to use it today: Darwinistically, materially. Race purity is a grotesque word in view of the fact that for centuries all stocks and species have been mixed, and that warlike—that is, healthy—generations with a future before them have from time immemorial always welcomed a stranger into the family if he had, 'race,' to whatever race it was he belonged."[7]

"The Fascist formations of this decade will pass into new, unforeseeable forms, and even present-day nationalism will disappear. There remains only the warlike "Prussian spirit—everywhere and not in Germany alone."[8]

The book was already in wide circulation and about 100,000 copies had been printed before the Nazi leadership awoke to its significance for their movement. Then they moved swiftly. Further circulation of *The Hour of Decision* was prohibited, and the German newspapers were forbidden even to mention the name of Spengler.

---

[6] Spengler, *The Hour of Decision*, Knopf, New York, 1934, p. 7.
[7] Ibid; p. 219.
[8] Ibid; p. 230.

The Man

On May 14, 1936, Oswald Spengler died suddenly in his bed from a massive heart attack. He died, as he had lived most of his life, in relative isolation. He was an austere, lonely figure. He had few friends and lacked a sense of humor or lightness of touch with which to attract others to him. In many respects, Spengler's personality reminds one strongly of the Old Testament prophets. Perhaps it was fortunate for him that he did not live any longer. Otherwise he might have ended his days behind the barbed wire of a Nazi concentration camp.

2

The Main Theme

THE SPENGLERIAN THEORY of cultural growth and decay is not difficult to understand provided two conditions are met. First, it is necessary to grasp the unusual meanings which the author attaches to certain key words. Second, one must brush aside the smoke screen of metaphysics with which he surrounds and beclouds his approach to the subject.

Spengler describes his work as a Morphology of History. By this he means the treatment of each separate culture as a living organism which is born, grows, decays and dies within the framework of a fixed and predictable life-cycle, just like any other living organism. He employs the word *Culture* to describe the living and creative phase of this organism, and *Civilization* as the end term of every culture, a period when all genuine creativity has disappeared, and the culture approaches its final demise under the bright glare of cold, abstract reason.[1]

[1]Spengler's use of the words *Culture* and *Civilization* was originated by

28

The next key-word encountered is *physiognomic*, the literal meaning of which is "pertaining to the face." Spengler uses it, however, to describe his intuitive approach to the problems of history;—looking directly into the face or the heart of historical events, rather than attempting to understand them by means of scientific analysis. Spengler also makes a rigorous distinction between two kinds of time. The first is the time of history, time as duration, which is irreversible, and which gnaws inexorably into the future. The second is the time of mathematical law, represented by the symbol *t*, which is reversible, and which is an abstraction from reality. The first relates to destiny and the second to the principle of causality.

These two concepts could lead us directly into the heart of Spengler's metaphysics, but discussion of this subject must be postponed until later in the study. At this point it will suffice to state that Spengler was convinced that the real essence of history could only be grasped by means of the physiognomic or intuitive approach.

In order to clear the ground for his theory of comparative cultures Spengler first launches a vigorous attack on the conventional classification of "Ancient," "Medieval" and "Modern" histories.[2] He describes this classification as "an

---

Nietzsche. There is a logic in this narrow definition of *Civilization* in that it is derived from the Roman word for *City*, and Spengler treats it as the period when all life is dominated by a few giant cities which drain the vitality of the surrounding countryside. Megalopolis is the word used by Spengler to designate these huge population centers.

[2]Eduard Meyer, in agreeing with Spengler's attack on the Ancient, Medieval and Modern categories, states that the tremendous expansion in the 19th Century of our knowledge of world history had already broken down the old concept into separate culture categories. No one prior to Spengler, however, had brought the problem into sharp focus.—Eduard Meyer, *Spengler's Untergang*; Berlin, 1925, p. 9.

incredibly jejeune and *meaningless* scheme," an egocentric conception of our western Culture which treats all past history merely as a backdrop to present day life in Europe. This conventional treatment of history is designated as the Ptolemaic system, in which all the other cultures are made to follow orbits around western Europe as the presumed center of all world events. Spengler describes his own method as the Copernican system which admits no priority in the treatment of any one culture in relation to all of the others.

Thus, in place of a linear concept of history leading up to and culminating in a picture of our own times, Spengler presents the story of eight separate High Cultures of the human race, no one of which is considered more important than any of the others. These eight are: the Babylonian, the Indian, the Chinese, the Egyptian, the Classical (the Culture of Greece and Rome), the Arabian (also called the Magian by Spengler), the West European (or Faustian) Culture, and finally the Mayan-Aztec Culture of Mexico.[3]

Each of these cultures is treated as a separate living entity with a definite limited life-cycle of approximately one thousand years, during which it actualizes all of the possibilities inherent in its own particular Weltanschauung (world-outlook). The civilization phase of a culture, however, may last for hundreds or even thousands of years more, while life continues in a kind of petrified state.

With this background one can grasp Spengler's idea of the birth and development of a culture, and of the contrast

---

[3]Spengler borrowed from Nietzsche the word "Apollinian" to define the Culture of Greece and Rome. Since he uses this term interchangeably with the word "Classical," the latter is used exclusively throughout this study.

between culture men and mankind as a whole. In one magnificent paragraph he sums up this philosophy:

"Mankind, however, has no aim, no idea, no plan, any more than the family of butterflies or orchids. 'Mankind' is a zoological expression, or an empty word . . . I see, in place of that empty figment of *one* linear history which can only be kept up by shutting one's eyes to the overwhelming multitude of the facts, the drama of a *number* of mighty cultures, each springing with primitive strength from the soil of a mother-region to which it remains firmly bound throughout its whole life-cycle, each stamping its material, its mankind, in *its own* image; each having *its own* idea, *its own* passions, *its own* life, will and feeling, *its own* death. . . . Each culture has its own new possibilities of self-expression which arise, ripen, decay, and never return. There is not *one* sculpture, *one* painting, *one* mathematics, *one* physics, but many, each in its deepest essence different from the others, each limited in duration and self-contained just as each species of plant has its peculiar blossom or fruit, its special type of growth and decline. . . . I see world-history as a picture of endless formations and transformations, of the marvelous waxing and waning of organic forms. The professional historian, on the contrary, sees it as a sort of tapeworm industriously adding on to itself one epoch after another."[4]

One may search the pages of the *Decline* in vain for a precise explanation of the birth of a culture; why it appeared, when and where it did, and why it emerged with its own particular world-outlook. It seems clear that Spengler

---

[4]Spengler, *The Decline of the West*; Vol. I, p. 21.

regarded these phenomena as part of the eternal mysteries of life: "A Culture is born in the moment when a great soul awakens out of the proto-spirituality of ever-childish humanity, and detaches itself, a form from the formless, a bounded and mortal thing, from the boundless and enduring."[5]

The author does throw some light, however, on the type of world-outlook that emerges in a particular culture by intimating that the surrounding landscape is a determining influence in shaping the soul of a culture. Thus, he sees in the hard, bright light of the Mediterranean a basic cause in shaping the Classical Culture, and the dark forests of northern Europe as a prime influence in shaping the brooding soul of Faustian man.

In the simplified and condensed explanation of Spengler's culture theories presented below, attention is concentrated very largely on only three of the eight cultures; the Classical, the Arabian or Magian, and the West European or Faustian, with occasional side glances at the others. Actually this was the course followed by Spengler himself. No one man could possibly have the breadth of knowledge sufficient to cover with equal facility and understanding all parts of the enormous area staked out in the *Decline*. The author was an accomplished Classical and West European scholar, with an adequate but more limited knowledge of the Magian and Egyptian Cultures. His understanding of the Babylonian, Indian and Chinese Cultures, however, was more superficial, and was practically non-existent in the case of the Mayan-Aztec Culture. As a result, a more understandable account can be presented by sticking closely to

[5]Spengler, *The Decline of the West*; Vol. I, p. 106.

the areas in which Spengler was most proficient. Moreover, the exposition in this chapter attempts only to cover the broad phases and turning points of the growth and decline of the several cultures.

The prime symbol of the Classical Culture was a concentrated concern with the *point-present,* the nearby and the small. The gods of Classical man were little more than human beings drawn in the large. His mathematics was the visible space geometry of Euclid. The architecture, as expressed in the Doric Temple, was wholly oriented to the external view, with its rows of columns and sculptured reliefs. The only interior was the simple cella, which was just large enough to house an heroic statue of a god or goddess, and which also faced to the exterior.

The primary art form of the Classical Culture was the free-standing nude statue of the human body. The typical nude statue was devoid of facial expression, designed deliberately to avoid revealing the personality of the original. Spengler points out that it was not until the late Roman period that human statues became at all biographical.

Classical painting, as revealed by the painted surfaces of the famous Greek amphorae or vases, was two-dimensional to a high degree, with almost no feeling of depth perception. "The Classical vase-painting and fresco—though the fact has never been remarked—has no time-of-day. No shadow indicates the state of the sun, no heaven shows the stars. There is neither morning nor evening, neither spring nor autumn, but *pure timeless brightness.*"[6] The human figures are highly stylized representations of warriors, maidens and sa-

---

[6]Spengler, *The Decline of the West;* Vol. I, p. 325.

tyrs. After studying a group of these vases, it is startling suddenly to come upon a Hellenistic portrait painting of the 1st Century A.D. and to realize that one is in a new world of art. Here one sees a portrait that is truly biographical, revealing clearly the personality and character of the original.

According to Spengler, Classical man was ahistorical, or lacking in any sense of or feeling for history. He could write brilliant accounts of contemporary events, such as Thucydides' *History of the Peloponnesian War,* or Xenophon's *Anabasis,* but anything of the remote past became transformed into myths, such as the Homeric legends. He had little appreciation of the reckoning of time and did not create an adequate calendar until the time of Julius Caesar. Classical man would have had no understanding whatsoever of our present day interest in archaeology. Thus, when the Acropolis was rebuilt after the Persian invasion of Xerxes, the Athenian citizens merely threw the remains of the former structures over the side of the hill into a massive dump heap.

The outstanding literary form of the Classical Culture was the drama, as exemplified in the great tragedies of Aeschylus, Sophocles and Euripides. These dramas were all, according to Spengler, "situation" tragedies, in which the protagonists were led to their destruction, not by their own deeds, but by the action of blind fate. Typical is the familiar story of Oedipus, which is not the tale of a hero struggling against alien forces and his own internal demons but one of a man who is led to his destruction by blind forces which he cannot attempt to combat.

An important feature of the Attic drama was its extreme formalism. Spengler points out that this effect was achieved deliberately in many different ways. In addition to the emphasis upon the so-called dramatic unities, the Greeks introduced the device of the chorus which largely dominated every scene. Masks, stilt-like shoes and padded clothing all combined to eliminate any possibility of individual characterization. This effect was further enhanced by monotonous sing-song speech delivered through a mouthpiece fixed in the mask. The result, according to Spengler, was exactly in keeping with the Attic spirit which prohibited all likeness-statuary.

The characteristic form of political organization of the Classical Culture was the Polis, or city-state—again an exemplification of the small and near. Instead of extending their frontiers by means of lateral expansion, Classical men established overseas colonies through maritime excursions. These colonies in turn became separate city-states, only loosely affiliated with the mother-city. This form of political organization was maintained rigorously throughout the Classical world and was only broken down by the emergence of the Roman Empire. Undoubtedly this spirit of separatism and exclusiveness was an important factor in causing the never-ending warfare amongst these small states.[7]

We turn now to a consideration of our West European, or Faustian Culture.[8] Here we find a soul which is diametri-

---

[7]As Toynbee has pointed out, the geography of the eastern Mediterranean may have influenced the development of the *Polis*. The typical Greek city was located on a small alluvial seacoast plain, and separated from the interior by a ring of mountains. The fact remains, however, that the form of city-state was adopted universally throughout the Classical world, and under conditions, such as those in Rome, when the above limitations to direct expansion did not exist.

[8]Spengler uses the word "Faustian" as a descriptive name for our West-European Culture. He finds in the limitless ambition of Goethe's *Faust* the perfect exemplar of the spirit of our Culture.

cally different from that of the Classical. Spengler calls it one of the great paradoxes of history that Faustian man should have developed such a cult of worship of the Classical Culture, which is so alien to him and which he has never really understood.

The prime symbol of the Faustian Culture is a limitless will-to-power and a reaching out into infinite space. Faustian man is as dynamic as Classical man was static, and every aspect of our Culture is an expression of this dynamism.

Out of the forms and symbols of Christianity, Faustian man created a new religion of his own, with Mary, the Mother of God, superseding Jesus as his principal deity. Spengler sees in Mary a symbol of care and of the Faustian feeling for time and history. As the Culture developed, the image of God, the Father, became more and more ethereal until it was almost identical with that of infinite space itself.

A counterpart to the adoration of Mary as the Queen of Heaven was an equally fervent belief in the constant nearby presence of the Devil and his cohorts. Spengler describes this duality as one of the most essential elements of the Gothic spirit and one which modern man is no longer capable of understanding. On the one hand, Gothic man saw Mary as a figure of utter beauty and tenderness, while, on the other, he felt himself surrounded by the realm of the Devil with his army of goblins, night-spirits, witches, werewolves, all in human shape. Spengler maintains that these two concepts were believed with a depth of sincerity that it is not possible to exaggerate, and that disbelief in either was deadly sin. "Man walked continuously on the thin crust of the bottomless pit. Life in this world is a ceaseless and desperate contest with the Devil, into which every individual plunges as a member of the church militant, to do battle for himself and to win his knight's spurs."[9]

In contrast to the static geometry of Euclid, the Faustian Culture produced the calculus, which is essentially the mathematics of motion. Spengler describes Faustian mathematics as dealing with functions and functional analysis rather than with concrete numbers. The creation of non-Euclidean geometries represented another step away from the Classical feeling for numbers. The culminating development, however, was the idea of multi-dimensional space which in turn led to the theory of Relativity.

The scientific interest of Classical man was almost wholly speculative, with little interest in experimentation and none whatsoever in technology. Faustian man, on the other hand, tested his scientific theories with experiments, and through these methods, developed a technology that was destined to overwhelm the whole world.

In architecture, the perfect expression of the Faustian spirit is the Gothic cathedral. As the Greek temple is wholly exterior, the Gothic cathedral can be appreciated only when viewed from within. The straining upward thrust of the mighty columns and pointed arches, the huge windows of coloured glass which impart to the outside light an ethereal quality, all combine to give one a feeling of reaching out into infinite space.

Although there have been many outstanding sculptors in our Culture, the material (with which the sculptor is forced to work) is too intractable to serve as an adequate vehicle to express the far ranging Faustian soul. Much better suited is

[9] Spengler, *The Decline of the West;* Vol. II, p. 289.

portrait painting which is not only biographical but also in its emphasis on depth perspective gives the impression of infinite space. But greatest of all the arts as an expression of the Faustian spirit is music, which transcends all temporal and spatial barriers and lifts man out of himself into the infinite.

The typical literary form of the Faustian Culture is the biography, either as the story of the life of an actual individual, or in the more popular form of the novel which developed later out of the biography. In either case we find a story, dynamic in character, of the development of individual human beings and of their struggles with forces outside of themselves as well as with demons within their own natures.

In drama Faustian man created a form of grand tragedy which was very different in character from the "situation" tragedies of the Classical world. In Shakespeare's *Macbeth* and Goethe's *Faust* we are dealing with individuals who display a limitless will-to-power, and who are led to their destruction, not by blind fate, but by their own deeds. "It is Time that is the tragic, and it is by the meaning that it intuitively attaches to Time that one culture is differentiated from another; and consequently "tragedy" of the grand order has only developed in the Culture that has most passionately affirmed (the Faustian), and that which has most passionately denied (the Classical), Time."[10]

Faustian man is historically minded to an extreme degree. His precise reckoning of time for centuries and millennia of the past, his invention of the clock in the 11th Century, his passion for archeology, are all facets of the same

---

[10]Spengler, *The Decline of the West*; Vol. I, p. 130.

spirit. Spengler saw a close relationship between the dynamic quality of the Faustian Culture and the historical spirit and asserted that to describe it as a dynamic culture is only another way of emphasizing the eminently historical character of its soul.

The characteristic form of political organization of the Faustian Culture is the nation state extending over a wide geographical area. Also, according to Spengler, the characteristic form of government is the dynastic monarchy. The Faustian feeling for time and care leads naturally to a strong desire for continuity and even perpetuation insofar as possible of the ruling family. The passionate devotion, almost a religion in itself, which Faustian man feels for his *Fatherland,* is a characteristic symbol of our Culture.

Spengler sees in parliamentarism and democracy merely a transitional stage between the dynastic monarchy and the coming of the Caesars. Where democracy becomes complete it lapses quickly into tyranny, as in the case of France in the last decades of the 18th Century. Parliamentarism works as an effective system of government only in those rare cases, such as in Great Britian in the 18th and 19th Centuries, where a powerful aristocracy manages, under the forms of democracy, to retain the control of government within its firm grasp. Even in the British example, however, Spengler sees clear signs of decay of parliamentarism by the end of the 19th Century.

When we turn to the Arabian or Magian Culture we find ourselves confronted by a culture that is not only different in form but also radically different in concept from all the others. The idea of a Magian Culture is the unique creation of Spengler himself. It is the outgrowth of the fact that there flowered in Asia Minor around the beginning of our Christian era a group of monotheistic religions which, though differing in dogma, had a common religiosity and a common world outlook. They are all the end results of several centuries of the teachings of prophets such as Amos, Isaiah, Jeremiah and Zarathustra.

Spengler saw in these prophetic teachings the birth of the Magian soul. Each of the prophets taught a belief in one god—Yahweh, Ahuremazda or Murduk-Baal—who represented the principle of good with all other deities being either impotent or evil. Along with this doctrine there arose the hope of a Messiah, first in the teaching of Isaiah, and then appearing everywhere during the next few centuries. This is the essence of the Magian religion, containing the idea of the historical struggle between good and evil in which the power of the good finally triumphs on the Day of Judgment. This moralization of history was basic in the religions of the Persians, the Chaldees and the Jews.

In its prime symbol, the Magian Culture emphasizes the cavern-like character of its world. *"The world of Magian mankind is filled with a fairy-tale feeling. Devils and evil spirits threaten man; angels and fairies protect him. There are amulets and talismans, mysterious lands, cities, buildings, and beings, secret letters, Solomon's seal, the Philosophers' stone, and over all this poured the quivering cavern-light that the spectral darkness ever threatens to swallow up."*[11]

This unceasing struggle between the forces of good and evil, with man as the center of the drama, permeates all as-

---

[11]Spengler, *The Decline of the West;* Vol. II, p. 237.

pects of the Magian Culture. There is something magical in algebra, a prime creation of Magian man, with its indefinite numbers and unknown quantities. Also essentially Magian is the Ptolemaic picture of the universe, with the earth at its center and surrounded by the cavern-like dome of the heavens.

Not only is Magian man's feeling for space radically different from that of the Classical or Faustian, but equally different is his feeling for time. Thus, Magian man was convinced that everything has a definite "time" from the origins of the Messiah, the hour of whose coming was set down in the ancient texts to the minor events of everyday life. Out of this belief emerged the early Magian astrology which assumes that all things are written down in the stars and that it is possible to foretell the course of human events by scientific calculations of the course of the planets.

In architecture, the closed-in space of the basilica and mosque is the perfect expression of the cavern-feeling: "Where the Egyptian puts reliefs that with their flat planes studiously avoid any foreshortening suggestive of lateral depth, where the Gothic architects put their pictures of glass to draw in the world of space without, the Magian clothes his walls with sparkling, predominantly golden, mosaics and arabesques and drowns his cavern in that unreal, fairy-tale light which for northerners is always so seductive in Moorish art."[12]

Most fundamental of all to the Magian world outlook is the conception of the state. In contrast to the Faustian idea of a fatherland, Magian man had no earthly home with a definite geographical location and clear-cut frontiers. In-

[12]Spengler, *The Decline of the West;* Vol. I, p. 200.

stead, he created the idea of the *consensus,* a nation of true believers in a particular religious faith no matter where they might be located geographically. This idea, so alien to western man, is expressed in the words of Jesus; "Wherever two or three are gathered together in my name, there will I be also."

The government of this Magian nation was also unique. In it the notion of a separation of the church and the state was unthinkable. The law of Magian nations is a law of creed-communities. In contrast to the laws of Classical and Faustian man which arose from practical experience, Magian man believed that all laws came directly from God who revealed them first to certain enlightened individuals. Such individuals in turn find the truth, not by personal pondering, but by ascertaining the general conviction of their associates which cannot err because the mind of God and the mind of the community are the same. If a consensus is found, truth is established.

According to Spengler, this idea of the *consensus,* unbounded by national frontiers, still permeates the Jewish race of today and accounts for the characteristic internationalism of this people. To Faustian man, with his deep-seated feeling for a fatherland, for which he is willing to fight and die, the idea of the consensus is utterly alien and incomprehensible.

Having covered in an abbreviated form the world outlook of three leading cultures, we turn now to a consideration of the life-cycles of these same cultures. Spengler dates the cultural, or living phase, of the Classical organism from about 1100 B.C. to about 100 B.C. The Magian Culture extends from about the birth of Christ to about 1000 A.D. and the Faustian from about 900 A.D. to about 1900 A.D.

Spengler asserts that pre-cultural man had no history in any proper meaning of that word. Such primitive people led a tribal and plant-like existence with an endless and meaningless repetition of births, struggles and death. The only important contribution of pre-cultural men, in Spengler's view, was the creation of a group of mighty legends and sagas which were the harbingers of the later births of the several cultures. Thus, the Classical Culture had its Homeric legends, the Faustian its Nibelungenlied and Viking sagas, and the Magian the utterances of its line of great prophets.[13]

In studying the history of the several high cultures it is essential to keep in mind three basic Spenglerian concepts. First, it is necessary to realize the unity of all the developments that unfold themselves in the life of each separate culture. At the core of the Spenglerian philosophy of history is the belief that the expression-forms of all branches of a culture are bound together in a tight morphological relationship. Thus, the religion, the mathematics, the architecture, the art forms, the philosophies, dramas and poetry, even the craftsmanship and choice of materials, are all expression-forms of the prime symbol of each separate culture. To understand fully the form-problems of history one must be aware of the unique character of such developments in each culture and of their close mutual relationships.

---

[13]As pointed out in Chapter I, Spengler realized later in life that he had left an important gap in his narrative of world history by his casual treatment of pre-cultural man. As a result, the study of pre-history became his most important concern during the last decade of his life.

The second concept is that each important stage in the youth, maturity and decay of each culture lasts for the same period of time as the similar stages in all of the other high cultures.

The third and final concept follows from the second. It is the idea that every important stage in the life of a culture is contemporaneous with a comparable period in all the other cultures. Thus, Spengler uses the word "contemporaneous" to mean, not the same date in a chronological calendar, but as referring to an event or stage in the development or decay of a culture which has its counterparts in similar periods in the life-cycles of all the other cultures.

Although the birth of a culture occurs in the pre-urban country-side, its history is largely one of the gradual urbanization of society. Thus, the developments of art and intellect are for the most part products of the cities. In the early stages of a culture this trend represents a normal and healthy growth. It is only in the late stages, when a culture has exhausted its potential for creativity, that one can see the sickness of society produced by the materialism of the giant cities of a dawning civilization which progressively drains all vitality from the surrounding country-side.

During the youth of a culture, two principal estates emerge—that of the nobility and that of the priesthood. The former are the fact men, the doers and the warriors, who act largely from a sure instinct. The priests, on the other hand, are the rationalizers and systematizers of life. In the Faustian Culture these two estates have engaged in a constant struggle with one another. It is, in Spengler's view, the fundamental conflict between the world-as-history represented by the nobility, and the world-as-nature represented by the

44

priesthood. Initially, this conflict is presented as a broad generalization as though it applied to all the cultures. Later Spengler makes clear that the situation he describes is applicable only to the Faustian Culture and that similar conflicts between the two estates did not appear in either the Classical or the Magian Culture.

The first great intellectual creations of a culture are the work of the priesthood. Such creations are known to us today as works of *scholasticism* and represent an attempt to rationalize the early religious beliefs. In the Faustian world this development culminated in the *Summa Theologia* of Thomas Aquinas, in which the author undertook to reduce the conduct of life to an exact science. His objective was the salvation of souls, and to this end he laid down rules of conduct based upon the Laws of God exactly as a modern scientist bases his conclusions upon the Laws of Nature. This intellectual structure dominated the thinking of the early Faustian Culture, and was only broken down by the emerging skepticism of the early lay scientists of the 16th and 17th Centuries.

In the Magian Culture, a comparable development is seen in the writings of the early church Fathers. This movement culminated in the *Civitas Dei* of St. Augustine, whom Spengler describes as "the last great thinker of Arabian Scholasticism, anything but a western intellect."[14] Because Augustine was purely Magian in his world outlook, his writings have always been a thorn in the flesh of western theologians who have struggled to reconcile his thinking with their own.

In the old age of a culture, as the importance of the lay

---

[14]Spengler, *The Decline of the West;* Vol. II, p. 241.

philosopher and scientist increases, and that of the priest diminishes, the latter is absorbed into a larger group of intellectuals in which the philosopher and the scientist play the leading roles. The importance of the nobility is similarly reduced and the nobles, as the *fact* men, are largely replaced by the entrepreneurs of business, and, to a lesser extent, by professional military leaders.

Spengler considers the peasantry as a non-estate. The plant-like existence of the peasants, with their close ties to the soil and the recurring cycles of weather, births and deaths, prevent them from taking any active part in the life of a culture. In the later stages of a culture, however, there emerges, in the city-dwellers or burghers, a third estate which grows steadily in importance as the culture matures and finally dominates the life of society. It is this class that carries through to fulfillment the various expression forms of a culture and leads in the transition from the cultural to the civilization stage of life.

A vital turning point in the life of a culture is the religious reformation which occurs *contemporaneously* in a fairly late phase of the life of every culture. In each case it is an effort to restore the religion to the purity of its original idea. For the Faustian world the reformation was largely the intellectual work of Luther and Calvin, and its most important outcome was the Puritanical Movement of Cromwell and his followers in England and Scotland. In the Classical Culture the reformation was led by Pythagoras and the Pythagoreans of the seventh and sixth centuries B.C. The Pythagorean revolt was fundamentally an effort to break away from the Olympian Pantheon of gods and to restore the early and simple worship of Demeter, the Earth

Goddess. It was also a Puritanical Movement and led amongst other things, to the destruction of Sybaris, the city of "all evil" in Italy.

In the case of Magian man, however, the reformation was nothing less than the emergence of Mohammed and the rise of Islam in the seventh century A.D. Spengler refuses to admit that Mohammedanism was a separate and distinct religion. "At most Islam was a new religion only to the same extent as Lutheranism was one. Actually, it was the prolongation of the great early religions. Equally, its expansion was not (as is even now imagined) a migration of peoples: proceeding from the Arabian Peninsula, but an onslaught of enthusiastic believers, which like an avalanche bore along with it Christians, Jews, and Mazdaists and set them at once in its front rank as fanatical Moslems. It was Berbers from the homeland of St. Augustine who conquered Spain, and Persians from Irak who drove on to the Oxus. The enemy of yesterday became the front-rank comrade of tomorrow. . . . The soul of the Magian Culture found at last its true expression in Islam."[15]

In all cases, Puritanism displayed a sober, pedantic kind of fanaticism, from which all the joy and humor of the early springtime religions had disappeared. In the Faustian world every Puritan, having become his own priest, carried within him his own personal Hell, as was vividly shown in Bunyan's *Pilgrim's Progress*. Similar sobriety and earnestness were shown in the ranks of the Pythagoreans and in the armies of the early Caliphs.

Puritanism was chiefly a movement of the urban middle class and was generally opposed by the nobility. With its

---

[15]Spengler, *The Decline of the West;* Vol. II, p. 304.

urban background the Puritan movement contained the seeds of rationalism which, after the passage of a few generations, burst forth everywhere. Puritanism was thus the prelude to the Age of Enlightenment. Locke in England, Voltaire in France, and Kant in Germany were the philosophic leaders of this development. In the Classical world a similar movement unfolded under the aegis of Socrates, Plato and Aristotle.

The 18th Century in Europe also witnessed a softening of the harsh fanaticism of the Puritan as a result of the emergence of the so-called Pietistic faiths, such as those of the Methodists and the Quakers. Under the growing influence of scientific materialism, there appeared concurrently the idea of god, the great watchmaker, who was believed to have started the machinery running and then to have left it to its own devices. In the Magian world the comparable and contemporaneous development of Pietism was known as Sufism.

In Spengler's view the principal art forms of the Faustian world reached their culmination in the 18th Century—the rococo in architecture, and the great contrapuntal creations of Bach, Mozart and Beethoven in music. He believed, however, that portrait painting had reached its apogee in the 17th Century with the work of Rembrandt. Western science, on the other hand, continued its free-wheeling advance throughout the 19th Century and, according to Spengler, only completed its basic thought structure in the early 20th Century.

In the Classical world, the work of Phidias and Praxiteles in Athens during the 5th Century B.C. marked the culmination of the art forms of this Culture. Classical science was largely speculative and the end term of this development is found in Archimedes.

A basic aspect of the transition of a culture to a civilization is the growing dominance of money and the rise of a class of capitalists and business entrepreneurs. In the Faustian world the beginning of the Industrial Revolution in the later 18th Century, accompanied by the philosophy of David Hume and Adam Smith, marked the emergence of the power of money.

When we turn to the Classical world, our scene shifts from Greece to Rome. Spengler asserts that a study of economics had no place in the small-scale life of the Greek cities. The history of Rome, however, is incomprehensible unless viewed from an economic standpoint. After the end of the second Punic War in the 3rd Century, B.C., there emerged in Rome a new class of capitalists that became more and more dominant during the following two centuries and culminated in such figures as Sulla, Pompey and Crassus. These men were the leaders in the unceasing warfare, chiefly civil conflicts, that took place during this period.

In a later chapter the difference in the concepts of Classical money and Faustian money is discussed in some detail. At this point it must suffice to point out that the Roman idea of wealth was a mass of concrete objects, such as gold and slaves. For late Faustian man, on the other hand, wealth arose out of credit or functional money created by the dynamism of business entrepreneurs.

According to Spengler, the power of money remains dominant during the early stages of a civilization but finally succumbs to what he terms the power of blood with the

49

coming of the Age of the Caesars. Thus, with the arrival of Julius Caesar and Augustus, the power of money was reduced to a subordinate role. It was the great capitalists of Rome who were responsible for the murder of Julius Caesar because they saw in him the beginning of the end of their power. In the Faustian world, however, we are still completely in the grip of a money economy.

Another important aspect of every late culture is the geographical expansion of its power and influence. For the Magian world, as we have already seen, this phenomenon appeared in the tidal waves of Islam which swept across north Africa into Spain and was finally checked by Charles Martel in southern France. Eastward the followers of Mohammed drove as far as the western borders of India.

The expansion of the more static Classical Culture was represented by a gradual extension of its power beyond the borders of the Mediterranean. This movement reached its limits in Spain in the west, England in the north, and Asia Minor in the east.

Most dramatic of all, however, has been the imperialistic expansion of the Faustian Culture. The early voyages of the Vikings were perhaps an early manifestation of this development. The real movement began, however, with the explorations of the Portuguese and Spanish navigators in the 15th Century and continued during the succeeding centuries with an ever rising tempo. Aided by improved navigational instruments and a vast superiority in military technology, Faustian man not only circumnavigated the globe, but also extended his power to its most remote corners.

The first stage of a *civilization* is the period of "contending states." This phase is marked by a succession of frightful wars and usually lasts for a century or more. At the end of the period an agonized and exhausted world accepts gratefully the coming of the Caesars who unite the warring factions and bring about an era of peace and stability.

The period of contending states for the Classical world was mentioned above. Spengler sees the 19th Century as a period of transition from the Faustian Culture phase to that of civilization. The true civilization starts in the 20th Century with the holocausts of World Wars I and II. If Spengler's view is correct, we are now right in the middle of our period of contending states and still fairly far removed from our Age of the Caesars with its prospective haven of security.

Spengler considers Alexander of Macedon and Napoleon as *contemporary* figures. He asserts, however, that both were romantic adventurers whose conquests left no permanent mark. They appeared just prior to the emergence of the civilization stage and their empires vanished within short periods of time leaving scarcely a ripple on the surfaces of their respective worlds.

The megalopolis is a prime symbol of every civilization. These giant cities dominate the life of their worlds and drain the vitality of the surrounding country-side. In the Classical world Rome was the one true megalopolis. In the Magian, Alexandria and Constantinople were comparable centers of population. Spengler sees in London, Paris, Berlin and New York the giant cities of our own civilization.

The inhabitants of the megalopolis are rootless, atheistic, and thoroughly materialistic. They erect giant structures, such as the Colosseum, the Pantheon, and the mighty Aqueducts of Rome, and the American skyscrapers of the Faustian world. All genuine creativity, however, has disappeared. In its place, a succession of schools and fads arise, flourish and quickly vanish.

An important characteristic of every megalopolis is the emergence of a new urban proletariat. In Rome this class consisted mainly of freed slaves as well as other immigrants from the outlying provinces. These people form a restless seething mass who are constantly threatening rebellion against the existing establishment. They are kept in check chiefly by liberal doses of *Bread and Circuses*, and by the modern equivalent in the form of welfare payments.

Another phenomenon of the late megalopolitan world is a gradual decline in population, despite a steady influx of fresh blood from outside. First, the nearby country-side is denuded of inhabitants by the magnetic attraction of the giant city. In these areas, agriculture practically disappears and food supplies are drawn from more and more remote sources. In the cities life continues to die out at the top. No longer is there pride in large families and in the succession of sons and heirs. This phenomenon is basically the result of a declining vitality of the urban population.[16]

In the Classical civilization Stoicism was the dominant philosophy, a calm and static acceptance of the vicissitudes of life. Spengler sees in socialism the dominant and more dynamic philosophy of the Faustian civilization. He defines

---

[16]The reader will find difficulty in reconciling Spengler's theory of a declining population in the civilization phase of a culture with the enormous population growth throughout the modern world, not only in the West but more spectacularly in the ancient civilizations of the Orient. The current population explosion is primarily the result of vastly improved methods of food production and advanced medical technology. Spengler, of course, was describing the situation that prevailed in the later periods of the Roman Empire, a stage from which we in the West are still far removed.

socialism more broadly than a mere belief in any particular political faith, or as a philosophy of human welfare. Instead, he sees it as an expression of the modern idea of "Progress," and the Faustian will-to-power. He states that the stoic takes the world as he finds it, but that the socialist wants to recast it in form and substance, to fill it with his own spirit.

In every late civilization there appears what Spengler calls "a second religiousness." This is a pallid revival of a belief in the religious symbols of the early culture. He makes clear, however, that there is no connection between this development and such modern cults as Christian Science and Theosophy, for which he expresses nothing but scorn.

As pointed out earlier, a civilization may last on for a millennium or more as a result of sheer size or relative isolation; for example, China and India. On the other hand, a civilization may be destroyed almost overnight by a brutal invasion. Such was the case when the tiny army of Cortez struck down the Aztec-Mayan Civilization in Mexico. The Magian Civilization was overwhelmed by a series of invasions by barbarians from the steppes of Asia. This movement reached its culmination when all of Asia Minor was occupied by the Ottoman Turks, and Constantinople fell at last to the invader in 1453 A.D.

The collapse of the Roman Empire resulted from a combination of the barbarian within and the barbarian without. The decline in the population of Italy forced Rome to replenish the depleted ranks of her far-flung legions with recruits from the nomadic tribes which were pressing against her frontiers. Thus, the defense of the Classical world passed gradually into the hands of its enemies. From this point it was an inevitable step to the takeover of the almost empty shell of the Empire by the Goths, the Ostrogoths and the Germans.

According to Spengler, the peoples of a late or destroyed civilization revert to a historyless existence. Their struggles and the rise and fall of various groups have become meaningless for the great panorama of world history. During the period of contending states, they fought, bled and died for ideals and rights without which life seemed not worth living. After the coming of the Caesars, however, these goals ceased to have any meaning. "A hundred years more, and even the historians will no longer understand the old controversies."[17]

Spengler uses the word "Fellaheen" to designate the people of a late or collapsed civilization. It is a term of contempt which was first employed to describe the Egyptians of the post-Roman period. It means a people without vitality, direction or destiny.

This summary exposition of Spengler's philosophy of history would not be complete without some comments on the literary organization of the work. A reader, on first approaching the *Decline,* is certain to be confused by the lack of any orderly presentation of the material. Thus, the author jumps abruptly from an opening chapter on mathematics to several chapters on his metaphysical assumptions, then back again to a discussion of the differences between cultures. Volume II opens with another lengthy metaphysical section, then moves into sections dealing with such di-

---

[17]Spengler, *The Decline of the West*; Vol. II, p. 432.

verse subjects as the megalopolis, the pseudomorphosis, the law, the religious reformations, the state, money and the machine, all presented without any apparent logical sequence. Throughout the whole work there is a constant turning back to previously discussed subjects, with the author repeating and amplifying his earlier statements.

It is only after a reader has lived with the *Decline* for some time that he begins to realize that the work has an order and logic of its own and that the repetitions and back-trackings fit into a unique literary pattern that is more the nature of a musical composition than it is that of a straight exposition. H. Stuart Hughes, in his book on Spengler, expresses this point of view eloquently: "Hence even the back-trackings and repetitions play their part, indeed are nearly indispensable, in the tightly woven, all interrelated effect that the author seeks to convey. Actually the *Decline* can hardly be said to start and end at any particular point. It is not to be read as a logical sequence. It is rather —to use the language of music to which Spengler was so deeply attracted—a theme and variations, a complex, contrapuntal arrangement, in which no one idea necessarily follows another, but in which a group of ideas, whose mutual relationship is symbolically experienced rather than specifically understood, summon, answer, and balance one another in the sort of lofty, cosmic harmony that Goethe's angels had proclaimed in the prologue and concluding stages of 'Faust.' "[18]

---

[18]H. Stuart Hughes, *Oswald Spengler*; Scribners, New York, revised edition 1962, p. 67.

3

The Critics and Successors

SPENGLER left himself open to attack on many fronts and his critics rushed in eagerly for the kill. In addition to straightforward intellectual criticism there was a strong emotional bias in many of his detractors: anti-German intellectuals who saw in the *Decline* a resurgence of the Prussian militaristic spirit, devout Christians who were shocked by his religious views, and a broad generality of individuals who were constitutionally incapable of accepting the idea of an inevitable decay of western civilization. So far as possible, the discussion in this chapter is restricted to unbiassed and intellectually honest opinions of critics, and to the broader aspects of such criticisms.

The most obvious point of attack for Spengler's critics was found in his concept of a culture as a living organism.

It is easy to understand why this idea became the object of widespread scorn. How can rational man accept the notion of a living higher organism arising out of the discrete thoughts and actions of a multitude of separate human beings?

Most readers of the *Decline* have been unable to swallow this radical concept except as an interesting and fruitful analogy. In fact, Spengler, in his humbler moments, tends to treat it in the same manner. Thus, on numerous occasions, he uses the word "analogy" to describe his method. "The means whereby to identify dead forms is mathematical law. The means whereby to understand living forms is analogy."[1] It seems doubtful, therefore, that he really intended this organic theory to be accepted literally.

About all that can be said positively with regard to the concept of a culture as a living organism is that culture men, particularly in the early stages of development, display a remarkable unity of thought and action, and tend to behave as though they were part of a higher organism. As a culture matures and decays, this unity becomes less and less apparent, and finally disappears. The extraordinary unity in an early cultural phase was illuminated beautifully in a letter of the 12th Century which Archbishop Hugo of Rouen wrote to Bishop Thierry of Amiens regarding the building of the Cathedral of Chartres:—

"The inhabitants of Chartres have combined to and in the construction of this church by transporting the materials; . . . they admit no one into their company unless he has been to confession, has renounced enmities and re-

---

[1]Spengler, *The Decline of the West*; Vol. I, p. 4.

venges, and has reconciled himself with his enemies . . . who has ever seen—who has ever heard tell, in times past, that powerful princes of the world, that men brought up in honour and in wealth, that nobles; men and women, have bent their haughty necks to the harness of carts, and that, like beasts of burden, they have dragged to the abode of Christ these waggons, loaded with wines, grains, oil, stone, wood, and all that is necessary for the wants of life, or for the construction of the church?"[2]

From his organic concept of cultures there follows logically Spengler's insistence that each culture is a more or less watertight compartment, the development of which is influenced by older cultures almost solely by the phenomenon of *pseudomorphosis.* Spengler employs this unusual word to describe those cases in which an older alien culture dominates a young culture to such an extent that the normal development of the latter is thwarted and distorted into senile expression-forms of the older culture. According to Spengler, an outstanding example of this phenomenon occurred during the period when the Roman Empire dominated the early springtime of the Magian Culture.

One can only agree with the critics that the idea of cultures as water-tight compartments and that of pseudomorphosis represent Spengler at his most dogmatic. Although each of these ideas seems to contain an important element of truth, it is clear that the author pushed both of them beyond the point where they can be accepted by an impartial observer.

Another prime example of Spenglerian dogmatism is seen in his insistence that each culture has a precise life-cycle of

[2]Quoted by Henry Adams, *Mont-Saint Michel and Chartres,* p. 104.

about one thousand years.[3] It is true he does qualify this concept at one point by describing it as the *ideal* life of one millennium for each culture as related to the ideal span of three-score years and ten for the life of an individual. In other words, in actuarial terms, the normal expectancy for the life of a culture is 1,000 years and 70 years for that of an individual, but the actual life spans of cultures and individuals may vary considerably from these norms. Nevertheless, throughout the *Decline* Spengler treats these cultural life-cycles with a rigidity that has been wholly unacceptable to his critics. Similar criticisms are applicable to the author's statements that each phase of the growth and decay of a culture is of precise duration, exactly equal to the time span of the same phase of other cultures.

A few general comments regarding Spengler's dogmatic exactitudes seem to be called for. The easiest explanation is that the author was so swept away by his biological metaphor that he could not resist carrying it to extremes beyond the limits of credibility. Another theory, however, should be mentioned. It will be recalled that one of the primary purposes behind the writing of the *Decline* was to demonstrate the author's ability to forecast the course of future events in our Faustian Civilization. Given this premise, it follows that the greater his ability to demonstrate exactly similar life spans for every culture and for the separate phases of each culture, the easier becomes his task of making accurate predictions of the future. Thus, consciously or unconsciously, Spengler may have been led into these rigidities in describing the past in order to strengthen his prophecies.

One ironic aspect of Spengler's predictions is that, in this

---

[3]Spengler, *The Decline of the West*; Vol. I, p. 110.

connection, he fell into a philosophic trap of his own making. Throughout the *Decline* the author emphasizes repeatedly his intuitive approach to history and his scorn for the use of the causality principle. Yet, in his professed ability to predict the future, he moves wholeheartedly over to the use of this same principle, apparently without being aware of the fact. Thus, a scientific law is nothing more than a model based upon observed recurrences in nature. As Spengler and many others have demonstrated, there can be no such things as laws of growth and change; there are only laws of recurrence which always assume that no new factor will enter the situation. It is obvious, therefore, that Spengler's ability to forecast the future rests solely upon the assumption that the rhythmic movement of past culture cycles will continue to repeat itself.

Another important area of criticism centers on the metaphysics of the *Decline*. At the outset it must be stated that, in this writer's opinion, the metaphysical aspect of Spengler's theories has been taken much too seriously by friend and foe alike. Thus, a careful analysis of the *Decline* makes it clear that the entire metaphysical superstructure can be shaken down to a few relatively simple assumptions arising out of the author's physiognomic or intuitive approach to history in contrast to the so-called "scientific" method of the positivist school of historians.

Examples of this superstructure are shown in the series of contrasting concepts developed by Spengler during the course of his study; destiny versus causality, time versus space, existence versus consciousness, totem versus taboo. These are all differing aspects of the author's emphasis upon the instinctive side of life and the intuitive approach to history in contrast to all efforts to intellectualize either life or history.

One of the first to recognize the relative insignificance of the metaphysical superstructure of the *Decline* was H. Stuart Hughes. In his book on Spengler he states that all of Spengler's pretentious metaphysics may be reduced to a clear and quite sensible distinction between systematic and physiognomic method. Hughes also asserts that most of the critics have failed to realize this distinction, and that their criticisms are applicable solely to "systematic" history, which is precisely the kind of history that Spengler was not attempting to write. "Fired by the discovery of some factual error, they have dashed off to meet him on a field of battle where he never had the slightest intention of putting in an appearance. Had the learned world read the *Decline* a little more carefully, the bulk of the controversy might never have occurred."[4]

Dr. Anton Koktanek, the director of the Spengler Archive in Munich, and author of *Oswald Spengler in Seiner Zeit*, agrees in general with Hughes. In a recent letter to this writer he stated that, in his creation of a metaphysical superstructure, Spengler was a true German. He then added; "Spengler's apparent metaphysical and philosophic argumentation was subjectively necessary in a people that from Leibniz through Kant, Fichte, Hegel, Schopenhauer, etc., believed to have perceived and mastered in philosophy the summit of knowledge and in metaphysics the summit of philosophy, where always a spiritual position above empiricism and rationalism was sought, and where an attack on a philo-

---

[4]H. Stuart Hughes, *Oswald Spengler*; Revised Edition, Scribners' N.Y., 1962, pp. 71–72.

sophical-metaphysical position must carry in its train a philosophical-metaphysical argument. I agree with Stuart Hughes in that essentially an understanding of Spengler may be reached without this philosophical-metaphysical element."

Somewhat paradoxically, many of Spengler's ciritics, after attempting to demolish his theories, have then turned to accuse him of having plagiarized his ideas from a long list of earlier writers. It seems necessary, therefore, to discuss briefly the intellectual background of Spengler's theories as well as his predecessors in the writing of cyclical history.

As stated earlier, the dominant intellectual forces in Spengler's life were Goethe and Nietzsche. On numerous occasions he gladly acknowledged his indebtedness to these two men. He declared that from the former he derived his method, and from the latter the questioning faculty.

Johann Wolfgang Goethe (1749–1832) has been described as the last great universal mind of our western civilization. Above all, he was a poet and dramatist of the first magnitude, second in stature perhaps only to Shakespeare. His far-ranging mind led him also into the fields of philosophy and science. Although never a systematic philosopher in the manner of Kant, Goethe's prose writings and voluminous correspondence are filled with philosophical observations. His scientific studies were devoted to optics and the morphology of plants. His approach was physiognomic or intuitive, in that he attempted to look directly into the heart of a problem. His interest lay almost wholly in organic or living nature, as opposed to the dead world of scientific law. It seems abundantly clear, therefore, that Spengler derived his intuitive approach to history and his organic theory of cultures directly from Goethe.

When we turn to Friedrich Wilhelm Nietzsche (1844–1900) we find a relationship that is much more complex. Superficially there are many parallels between the lives of Spengler and Nietzsche. Both were solitary, lonely men who lived out their lives as bachelors. Both were tormented constantly by migraine headaches, and each had a life span of just 56 years. Both were profound students of Classical antiquity, with particular reverence for Heraclitus from whom they derived the idea that "war is the creator of all things." Both men had a deep love of music and poetry, and the poetical quality of Nietzsche's writing was undoubtedly an important factor in its appeal to Spengler.

That Spengler had an intimate knowledge of Nietzsche's works and derived many of his ideas from this source is attested by the fact that the first volume of the *Decline* contains 46 separate references to Nietzsche. It is surprising to note, however, that at least half of these references are critical, whereas there is not one uncomplimentary comment about Goethe.

Spengler's criticisms of Nietzsche are based upon his conviction that the latter was essentially a romantic who believed he was writing for all mankind and who never realized that his concepts of morality and will-to-power were applicable solely to Faustian man. Thus, Spengler accuses Nietzsche of never having moved out of the traditional scheme of "Ancient," "Medieval" and "Modern" history. He also observes that Nietzsche never succeeded in placing himself "beyond good and evil." "He tried to be at once sceptic *and* prophet, moral critic *and* moral gospeller. It cannot be done. One cannot be a first-class psychologist as long as one is still a romantic. And so here, as in all his crucial penetrations, he got as far as the door—and stood outside it."[5]

Finally, Spengler saw in Nietzsche's break with Wagner and his unconscious step from Schopenhauer to Darwin a harbinger of the beginning of the civilization phase of the Faustian Culture. He describes this change as a shift from the metaphysical to the physiological expression of the same world feeling and that Nietzsche's "will-to-power" was merely another name for Darwin's "struggle for existence."

"But Nietzsche was also a socialist without knowing it. Not his catchwords, but his instincts were socialistic, practical, directed to that welfare of mankind that Goethe and Kant never spent a moment upon. Materialism, Socialism and Darwinism are only superficially and on the surface separable."[6]

Yet, despite these criticisms, Spengler felt a deep reverence for Nietzsche and clearly regarded him as one who had prepared the way before him and thus assisted him in arriving at his theory of separate living cultures. In his address on the occasion of the 80th anniversary of Nietzsche's birth, Spengler summed up his feeling with the statement that Nietzsche was the first to recognize that history was not just the story of a series of events but that all cultures, periods, races have a soul development like individual people, and that this was an enormous step forward in historical understanding. When Spengler died in 1936 his family placed in his coffin two books—one, a copy of Nietzsche's

[5]Spengler, *The Decline of the West*; Vol. I, p. 346.
[6]Ibid; Vol. I, p. 370.

Also Sprach Zarathustra; and the other, a copy of Goethe's *Faust.*

Brief mention must now be made of three other writers from whom Spengler has been frequently accused of deriving many of his ideas. At the outset it should be stated that the evidence, both internal and external, indicates clearly that Spengler was unacquainted with their works.

The first of these is Giambattista Vico, an obscure Italian scholar and teacher who, in the first half of the 18th Century, wrote a book which was finally translated into English two centuries later with the title *The New Science.*[7] In this work Vico displayed a vivid comprehension of the cyclical nature of history and the rise and fall of civilizations. Taking his examples almost entirely from the history of Greece, Rome and Egypt, he sets forth three general stages in the history of nations or civilizations. The first is the divine or theocratic, in which men believed that everything was commanded by the gods. The second is the heroic or aristocratic stage in which all power resides in a ruling class of nobles. The third is that of popular or democratic governments. Finally, Vico asserts that all popular governments become corrupt and fall into the perfect tyranny of anarchy which is the worst of all tyrannies. As a devout Christian, however, Vico was unable to predict the decay of our western civilization. Like Toynbee two centuries later, he believed that we would be saved from this fate by the strength of the Christian religion.

---

[7] Reprinted from Thomas Goddard Bergin and Max Harold Fisch: THE NEW SCIENCE OF GIAMBATTISTA VICO: Revised Translation of the Third Edition (1744). Copyright © 1968 by Cornell University, copyright © 1961 by Thomas Goddard Bergin and Max Harold Fisch, copyright 1948 by Cornell University. Used by permission of Cornell University Press.

Written in a somewhat obscure style, *The New Science* remained relatively unknown for 150 years until it was brought to light around the end of the 19th Century by Benedetto Croce, the Italian philosopher and historian. Even then a knowledge of this book was limited largely to the circle of serious students of Croce. In fact, Vico did not become widely known until after the publications of the works of Spengler and Toynbee when his book became "must" reading for all students of cyclical history.[8]

Although it was brought to his attention later, there is no reason to believe that Spengler had ever heard of Vico when he wrote the *Decline*. It seems evident that had Spengler been familiar with *The New Science*, he would have clasped Vico to his bosom as one of the first to have a vision, albeit somewhat naive, of the rise and fall of civilizations. In just such a manner did Spengler revere the memory of the 12th Century Abbott, Joachim of Floris, who introduced the time spirit into religion by classifying history into the Age of the Father, the Age of the Son and the Age of the Holy Ghost.

Our second predecessor is a Russian scientist, Nikolai Danilevsky (1822–1885). Although trained as a botanist, Danilevsky's wide-ranging mind led him to writings in many different fields, including Darwinism, economics, political science and linguistics. In 1869 he published, in Russian, a book entitled *Russia and Europe,* which is startlingly similar in its approach and in its contents to the historical theories of Oswald Spengler. Just like Spengler, Danilevsky repudiates the traditional "Ancient," "Medieval," and

---

[8]It is interesting to note that Karl Marx, in *Das Kapital,* does make a reference to Vico's work.

"Modern" classification of history as an egocentric concept of western Europe. Then, in place of Spengler's eight High Cultures, he delineates what he terms ten different historico-cultural types or civilizations as follows: (1) Egyptian, (2) Chinese, (3) Assyro-Babylonian-Phoenician-Chaldean or Ancient-Semitic, (4) Hindu, (5) Iranian, (6) Hebrew, (7) Greek, (8) Roman, (9) Neo-Semitic or Arabian, (10) Germano-Romanic or European. Despite minor differences, one can see at a glance the close similarity between this classification and that of Spengler. Moreover, both writers saw in Russia an emerging new culture.

With his background in botany, it was only natural that Danilevsky's treatment of civilizations should be morphological, much like that of Spengler, but without the latter's metaphysics. Thus, Danilevsky describes the influence of one civilization upon another either as a process of grafting or of cross-fertilization but points out that such influences are not likely to be significant or lasting

Finally, Danilevsky answers the question as to the reason for the permanent hostility between western Europe and Russia. The answer, of course, is that the two are alien civilizations and that the former is some 500 years ahead of the latter in its development.

Russia and Europe is unquestionably a brilliant piece of work and places its author in the front ranks of the cyclical school of historians. There is no evidence, however, that Spengler had ever heard of Danilevsky prior to the publication of the *Decline*. The book achieved a widespread popularity in Russia largely because of its Slavophil character. Outside of Russia, however, it remained practically unknown for a full half century, until it was translated into

German in 1920 because of the popularity of the *Decline* and the similarity between the two works. Finally, the evidence is clear that Spengler did not possess a knowledge of Russian that would enable him to read this work prior to its translation into German.[9]

Our third predecessor is the French philosopher Henri Bergson (1859–1941). In this case we are dealing with a man who was not an historian but wholly a philosopher. His master work *L' Evolution Creatice* was published in 1907 and had a tremendous impact throughout the western world.[10] The significance of Bergson for Spengler lies in the fact that the latter's distinction between time as duration and mathematical time, his definition of scientific law and organic life, and the necessity of understanding organic life solely by means of an intuitive approach are almost identical with the ideas expressed earlier by Bergson. Even in his discussion of mathematics and physics, Bergson's treatment bears a close resemblance to that of Spengler. Thus, he contrasts ancient geometry, which was purely static, with modern geometry, which studies the varying of a function. Also, like Spengler, he describes the second law of thermodynamics, or entropy, as the most metaphysical of all the laws of physics since it merely describes the direction in which the world is going.

In the case of Bergson we have a specific statement by Spengler that, although he had heard of the man, and had read one brief anti-German pamphlet by him, he was entirely unacquainted with his philosophic writings. As far as internal evidence is concerned, it is unthinkable that Speng-

---

[9]N. I. Danilevsky, *Russland Und Europa;* Stuttgart. 1920.
[10]Henri Bergson, *Creative Evolution,* Henry Holt, N. Y., 1923.

ler, in making the distinction between time as duration and mathematical time, if he had read Bergson, could have stated that this represented "an opposition that has never yet been noted."[11]

The three writers discussed above provide excellent examples of the truth that in the course of human events there is a "time" for almost all developments. By this is meant, not time in the Chaldean sense of being foretold in the stars, but rather a fullness or ripeness of time. Most of us are familiar with the fact that new ideas or new inventions, if developed prematurely, often lie dormant for many years before finding general acceptance. A classic case is that of the Austrian Monk, Gregor Mendel, who discovered and formulated the laws of heredity in 1866 but who remained almost unknown until the end of the century. A similar fate was experienced by both Vico and Danilevsky.

It is also well known that, when the time is ripe, two or more thinkers frequently develop the same ideas at the same time and entirely independently of each other. Such was clearly the case of Bergson and Spengler. The latter stated that his theories were called for in the second decade of the 20th Century, and at no earlier time.

With regard to more specific criticisms of Spengler, we turn first to the comments of Eduard Meyer, the distinguished German historian of antiquity. Although Meyer was one of the few early supporters of Spengler of professional stature, his book on the *Decline* contains numerous criticisms of the author's theories.[12] Perhaps the most important of these is his repudiation of Spengler's whole concept

---

[11]Spengler, *The Decline of the West;* Vol. I, p. 6.
[12]Eduard Meyer, *Spengler's Untergang de Abendlandes;* Berlin, 1925,

of a Magian Culture. After admitting the value of Spengler's thesis of a Magian nation as a consensus of believers without a geographical home, Meyer proceeds to demonstrate that the whole area is too large and diverse to be covered by one culture, and goes too far back in time to fit Spengler's pattern. He also states that Islam was not just a puritanical movement in the Magian soul but was something entirely alien and independent. Certainly Meyer was correct in pointing out that Spengler's Magian Culture was very different in structure, particularly as far as homogeneity is concerned, from the other high cultures. Nevertheless, it has always seemed to this writer that the concept of a Magian Culture is one of the most fruitful products of Spengler's historical imagination.

Meyer also insists that Rome represents a culture separate and distinct from that of Greece and that the profound influence of Hellenism upon Rome can be described more accurately as an example of Spengler's theory of pseudomorphosis. The only comment necessary in connection with this statement is that one could just as easily treat the United States of America as a different culture from that of western Europe.

Amongst other minor criticisms, Meyer asserts his disagreement with the Spenglerian theory that Classical man was ahistorical. He does this largely on the ground that large groups in Greece and Rome, from the time of Plato and Aristotle were aware of their decline and were, therefore, historically minded. Perhaps so, but it seems undeniable that the lack of classical interest in its remote past displayed an attitude radically different from the extreme concern shown by Faustian man for an accurate recreation of past history.

Outside of Germany, the *Decline* was greeted by a hostile reception by most professional critics. In France it produced a strange book by the French historian, André Fauconnet.[13] After presenting an unusually lucid, and apparently sympathetic exposition of Spengler's thesis, the author turns at the end and dismisses him as a chauvinist, chiefly because of Spengler's innocent statement, in the preface to the second edition of the first volume, that he hoped his work would be recognized *as a German philosophy.*

In Great Britain the attack on the *Decline* was led by the historian, H. G. Collingwood, who repudiated the whole theory of separate cultures. In the United States most of the professional critics joined in the attack. Practically the only voice of professional standing raised in support of Spengler was that of the historian Charles Beard, who wrote:

"Even if most of his analogies are indefensible and his conclusions wrong, still his *Decline* is a great work—one of the few mighty books of our time—mighty in its challenges, in its psychological analysis, in its efforts to grasp at the hem of destiny. On almost every page there are sentences of sharp cutting power, which alone make the labor of reading it rich in rewards."[14]

Probably the best and most succinct summary of the whole Spengler controversy was written by Manfred Schrö-

---

[13]André Fauconnet, *Un Philosophe Allemand Contemporain: Oswald Spengler,* Paris, 1925.

[14]Quoted on flyleaf of *Man and Technics* by Oswald Spengler in the English edition by Knopf N. Y. 1932 and reissued 1963.

ter.[15] In discussing the attack on Spengler's view of art by the Egyptologist Curtius, Schröter points out that each of the two takes an opposite and equally dogmatic approach to the subject—Spengler emphasizing the cultural differences, and Curtius emphasizing the fundamental unity of all mankind. Schröter then maintains that these two views should not be mutually exclusive but complementary. The basic question then becomes not whether Spengler's approach is completely right or wrong, but whether it is fruitful and enlightening.

During the years since the appearance of the *Decline* a series of historians has emerged who have adopted the cyclical approach to the writing of history. No one of these has agreed with any of the others as to the proper methods to be employed, but all have agreed in their disagreement with those used by Oswald Spengler.

By all odds the most important of these later writers has been the British historian, Arnold Toynbee. Between the third and fifth decades of this century, Toynbee produced his monumental *Study of History* in 12 massive volumes. Fortunately, an excellent two volume abridgement of the original has been written by D. C. Somervell. Yet even the abridgement runs to almost one thousand pages. This writer must confess that, after agonizing through the first four volumes of the *Study*, he gave up the attempt and resorted to the abridgement.

At the outset it should be emphasized that Toynbee did not derive his ideas from Spengler. Instead the work was the result of 40 years of independent research. The author did

---

[15]Manfred Schröter, *Der Streit um Spengler;* Munich, 1922, p. 50.

confess later that, after first reading the *Decline*,[16] he had grave doubts as to the wisdom of proceeding with his own study. He finally decided to do so because he realized that his approach to the subject was so different from that of Spengler.

Fundamentally what Toynbee attempted to do was to develop a theory of the rise and fall of civilizations without resort to metaphysics and without the Spenglerian idea of the organic character of the separate cultures. In place of this approach, he introduced his own original concept of Challenge and Response. Thus, a civilization arises out of primitive society when a people makes a successful response to an unusual challenge in its environment.

Toynbee makes the most effective use of this concept in his description of the birth of the Egyptian civilization. When the recession of the latest Ice Age produced a progressive desiccation of the North African littoral, the nomadic tribes in this area were confronted by two alternative choices. One group moved south to the equatorial regions of the upper Nile—and remained primitives. The other group invaded the thickets and swamps of the lower Nile and carved out a sedentary agrarian society through the development of irrigation. It was the effective response of the latter group to the challenge that gave rise to the Egyptian civilization. Similar examples are presented for the birth of the Sumeric civilization in the deltas of the Tigris and Euphrates Rivers, and for the Chinese civilization in the lower regions of the great rivers of China.

In place of Spengler's eight High Cultures, Toynbee de-

[16]Arnold Toynbee, *Civilization on Trial*, Oxford University Press, New York, 1948, pp. 9–10.

73

lineates 21 separate civilizations. In elaborating his theory of Challenge and Response, the author asserts that each successful response to a challenge produces in turn a new challenge which must be surmounted. Toynbee points out that these challenges may be environmental, they may take the form of military aggressions by outsiders or by the civilization itself, and even may be spiritual or religious in character. The growth of a civilization covers that period when it is achieving successful responses to its succession of challenges, and its decline begins when it fails to make an effective response to its most recent challenge.

In addition to his list of 21 complete civilizations Toynbee includes several arrested civilizations such as that of the Eskimos and that of the Polynesians. In the former case the author sees an environmental challenge so severe that having met successfully the initial challenge by finding a way of survival in the Arctic, the Eskimo society was unable to proceed farther up the ladder of civilization. In the case of the Polynesians Toynbee maintains that, having surmounted their first hurdle by a successful trans-Pacific migration, they found in their new environment no challenges sufficient to stimulate additional progress. From these examples it follows that challenges must be neither so severe as to crush the growth of a nascent civilization nor so mild as to provide insufficient stimulus for further growth. What is called for in the realm of challenges is a golden mean which will furnish just the right degree of stimulus to a vigorous society and yet will not destroy it entirely.

Undoubtedly it would be horrifying to Toynbee to learn that his treatment of warfare bears any resemblance to Spengler's dictum that "War is the creator of all things."

Yet, if Spengler's statement were rephrased to read—"Adversity, of which war has always been one of the most important causes, is the creator of all things," it would be a close approximation to Toynbee's theory of Challenge and Response.

Toynbee finds no close similarity in the time periods of the growth phase of different civilizations but he does admit that such time similarities exist in the disintegrating phase of civilizations. In fact, his whole treatment of declining civilizations comes fairly close to that found in the *Decline* —the loss of a sense of direction; the disappearance of religious values; a time of troubles covering several centuries of enervating civil wars and wars between parochial states; and finally the emergence of a Universal State, which corresponds very closely to Spengler's *Civilization*. In the Universal State Toynbee sees an external proletariat, consisting of the barbarians pounding at the gates, and an internal proletariat made up of depressed and dissident groups who are constantly attempting to overthrow the dominant minority. During the growth phase of a civilization this latter group was the creative minority; later it loses its creative powers and spends all its energies in attempting to maintain its position in the social structure.

In all his writing Toynbee displays an air of reasonableness that is very beguiling to the reader. As his various themes unfold, however, one runs into a series of sweeping generalizations which in their own way are fully as dogmatic as those of Spengler. Thus, Toynbee's highly fruitful concept of Challenge and Response is pushed by the author beyond the breaking point of credibility. Practically every important historical event is treated as a challenge of some

75

kind and many of the indicated responses appear extremely farfetched.

Moreover, Toynbee never succeeds in explaining why one civilization is more successful than others in meeting its challenges, except negatively in the extreme cases of the so-called arrested civilizations. At one point Toynbee asserts that the more vigorous and successful societies have a greater *élan vital* than others.[17] Either this is a tautological statement or else it must be based upon metaphysical presuppositions.

Toynbee also introduces a second basic concept in his study which remains somewhat baffling. This is his idea of Withdrawal and Return. With reference to the lives of individuals, such as Jesus and Mohammed, it is easy to understand the meaning of the concept. When, however, Toynbee attempts to make it applicable to the lives of civilizations we are confronted with something very different. Here we have either a non-sequitur, or else an idea with definite metaphysical overtones. Fortunately, while this concept figures prominently in the early part of the study, it disappears almost entirely in the later parts.

Toynbee came to his task with a vast erudition, particularly in the fields of political, military, economic and religious history. His great lack, however, was in the history of the arts and sciences, wherein lay one of Spengler's greatest strengths. Toynbee refused to admit any symbolic significance in these expression forms as indicative of the differences among the separate cultures. His comments about the arts are scattered, perfunctory, and frequently irrelevant. In

[17]D. C. Somervell, *Abridgement of a Study of History*; Oxford Univ. Press, Vol. I, p. 187.

fact, he is guilty of making the extraordinary statement that the genesis of the Gothic cathedral was the result of observations by the Crusaders of similar edifices in Syria and brought back by them to western Europe.[18]

Above all else Arnold Toynbee is a devout Christian believer, and this characteristic shines out brightly throughout his entire work. Although he admits the widespread evidence of decay in our western civilization and acknowledges that all previous civilizations have gone the way of all flesh, his faith that Christianity is something above and distinct from all earlier higher religions prevents him from predicting an inevitable disintegration of our own civilization. As a result, like Vico's work two centuries earlier, *A Study of History* tends to become more of a history of salvation than a comparative study of civilizations. In one important section Toynbee actually reverses his method and considers civilizations as outgrowths of the higher religions instead of treating the religions as products of such civilizations.

One need not go so far as to agree with the facetious remark of one critic who stated that Toynbee's conclusions imply a belief that, if everyone joined the Church of England, the future would be assured. Nevertheless, one must agree that Toynbee's piety detracts from his objectivity and tends to reduce his stature as a writer of cyclical history.

As a piece of literature, *A Study of History* cannot be compared to the dramatic sweep of the *Decline*. Its style is pedestrian and somewhat pedantic, and the author's tendency to jump back and forth rapidly from one civilization to another makes the exposition somewhat difficult to fol-

---

[18]D. C. Somervell, *Abridgement of a Study of History;* Oxford Press, 1957, Vol. II, p. 193.

low. Nevertheless, Toynbee's relative optimism and deep religious faith have given the work a widespread popularity with the general public.

Finally, it cannot be denied that, despite its shortcomings, *A Study of History* is an important work and a valuable contribution to an understanding of human history. Also it serves as an excellent antidote to the excesses of Spengler, and a reading of both works tends to bring about something of an intellectual balance between the divergent views. Toynbee's *Study* contains many brilliant passages which are richly rewarding. This seems particularly true of his treatment of the problems of modern western civilization. Thus, his discussion of the baneful influence of the present religion of nationalism is excellent. Another small example is seen in his description of the problems facing a great industrial nation in waging a guerrilla war against a primitive people which has obtained the use of modern weapons. Although written chiefly to explain the problems which confronted the British in their attempts to subdue the hill tribes along the northwest frontier of India, it could serve as a textbook description of the difficulties which have plagued the United States in Vietnam.[19] Also first rate is Toynbee's exposition of the emergence of Russia and the United States as the two surviving great powers, and the resulting problems for the nations of western Europe.

Two other later writers of cyclical history deserve brief mention. One is a Russian sociologist, Pitrim A. Sorokin, who published, between 1937 and 1941, a four volume work entitled *Social and Cultural Dynamics*. The second is

---

[19]D. C. Somervell, *Abridgement of a Study of History*; Oxford Press, 1957, p. 128.

an American anthropologist, Alfred L. Kroeber, whose book *Configurations of Culture Growth* appeared in 1944.

These two writers display many similarities in their methods as well as important differences. Both reject the ideas of Danilevsky, Spengler and Toynbee that human history can be segregated into definite and distinct cultures or civilizations. Instead, they insist that smaller social units, usually nation states, represent the proper field for investigation. Also both writers make extensive use of statistics to verify their conclusions.

The differences between Sorokin and Kroeber are revealed when the former moves away from analysis of smaller social units to a discussion of much larger cultural groups which he designates as supersystems, and which come fairly close to Spengler's concept of separate cultures. Sorokin classifies these supersystems into three different types—the *Sensate*, the *Ideational* and the *Idealistic*. A Sensate society is described as one in which the dominant philosophy or Weltanschauung determines that the ultimate true reality-value is based upon sensory perception and beyond this there is no other reality nor any other non-sensory value. An Ideational society is one in which the ultimate and only true reality-value is a supersensory and super-rational God. The Idealistic society is one in which the sensory and rational perceptions are combined with the super-rational-supersensory to form a mystical and harmonious unity.

As an example of an Ideational society, Sorokin cites the Medieval European culture from the sixth to the end of the twelfth century. During this period the supreme truth was the revealed truth of the Christian religion which dominated

79

all aspects of life—philosophy, science, art, economics and government.

Sorokin then points out that, from the sixteenth century to the present day, European society has become progressively secularized. God and religion have tended to fall by the wayside and the real truth has become the truth of the senses, empirically perceived and tested. This attitude has pervaded all aspects of society to a point where modern European culture is now dominated by the Sensate supersystem.

Finally, Sorokin saw in the Greek society of the fifth century B.C., a culture that was dominated by the Idealistic supersystem. Thus, the Greek culture found the true, ultimate reality in a harmonious combination of sensory, rational, superrational and supersensory values.

Kroeber, on the other hand, confines his analysis to smaller cultural units, usually nation states. One of Kroeber's principal methods is an attempt to sort out statistically what he terms "Clusters of Genius" in the fields of philosophy, science, art, etc. In this analysis Kroeber finds little evidence of regular periodicity in the rise and decline of societies. To say the least, an effort to classify genius statistically is a highly questionable technique. Although Kroeber's common sense saves him from such an error, the logic of this method could easily result in absurdities, because there is no common yardstick for measuring the quality of genius.[20]

Despite the wide differences in the approach, and in the

---

[20]Sorokin also has criticized Kroeber's method of studying genius. The former points out that the latter considers the problem solely from the viewpoint of the modern Sensate supersystem, and that Kroeber fails to recognize that, during the Ideational phase of the early Medieval period, many creative geniuses

methods employed, it is surprising to discover that both Sorokin and Kroeber end up with philosophies of history not
very different from that of Spengler. In a more recent book
Sorokin expressed this fundamental agreement as follows:

"All this means that each basic assumption of culture or
civilization has its own system of truth, beauty, and good-
ness; its own type of science, philosophy, painting or music,
literature or architecture, ethics or politics, dissimilar from
these of another, substantially different cultural supersystem. . . These authors (Danilevsky, Spengler, Toynbee,
Kroeber, etc.) have demonstrated this cultural determination and molding of all "mental products" beyond a reason-
able degree of doubt . . . largely as a result of their labor we
now know that even a mathematical number does not mean
the same in essentially different cultures, not to mention sciences, philosophies, religious beliefs, ethical norms, even
technological gadgets and what not. So far as they are in-
gested by a cultural supersystem (and some forms are vigorously rejected) they are all modified and transformed in the
image of the superstructure."[21]

Kroeber for his part arrived at a similar conclusion when
he wrote:

"Apparently when a given civilization breaks through to
the philosophic level, it brings to this a particular body of
knowledge, a particular group of religious assumptions, a
particular set of social institutions. Out of these it develops
something new; its particular system of philosophy . . . such

in philosophy, science, and the arts remained anonymous because of the dominating influence of religion.
P. A. Sorokin, *Modern Historical and Social Philosophies,* Dover Publications,
New York, 1963, p. 264.
[21]Ibid, p. 307.

a system bears in itself certain specific potentialities, and also specific limitations, which enable, even compel it, barring catastrophe from outside, to realize or fulfill itself to the terminus of these potentialities, but not to go beyond them. When a given set of potentialities is exhausted, the growth ends. . . "

"This view is likely to be construed as savoring of the mystic, because of the element of predestination—even though limited and specific predestination—which it contains, and for its analogy to the phenomena of organic growth. I regret this, but cannot help it: the empirical phenomena, over and over again, and with remarkably few exceptions compel the conclusion that there are whole arrays of events in the history of culture which are objectively describable only in terms of the metaphors of "growth," "realization," "exhaustion," and "death," as our vocabulary today stands."[22]

There can be no doubt that the group or school of cyclical historians, running from Danilevsky through Kroeber, and including many others not mentioned herein, has had a tremendous impact upon modern thought. Today these ideas are accepted as respectable and commonplace as compared with the furore created when *The Decline of the West* was first published. Although the theories of cyclical history are still far from finding universal acceptance amongst professional historians, these ideas are continuing to gain ground with thoughtful students.[23]

---

[22]Kroeber, *Configurations of Culture Growth;* Univ. of Calif. Press, 1944, pp. 90–91. Reprinted by permission of The Regents of the University of California.

[23]An excellent example of a writer who still clings to the lineal theory of history is to be found in William H. McNeill's, *The Rise of the West*, published in 1963. The author presents a straightforward, and very readable story of

human history, chiefly in terms of political, military and economic developments. He traces the development of humanity from its earliest beginnings to its culmination in our western civilization with a technology that now dominates the earth. Although the last chapter expresses some doubts as to the continuing viability of our civilization, the book as a whole, including its title, is a clearcut effort to refute the Spenglerian thesis of decline.

4

Oswald Spengler Today

THE BASIC OBJECTIVE of this study is to examine Spengler's predictions of a decline of our western civilization after the passage of a half century. The three preceding chapters have been designed to provide a background of understanding for readers not intimately familiar with the Spenglerian philosophy of history. This chapter, however, brings us to the heart of the problem. At the outset it should be noted that, while the background material has been presented as objectively as possible, the conclusions set forth herein are strictly my own, with which readers are free to agree or disagree. I can only hope they will find them interesting.

My first general conclusion is that there is nothing logically inevitable about a decline of western civilization. Spengler's doctrine of inevitability rests solely upon the assumption that, because such a fate has overtaken all earlier civilizations, our own must necessarily follow the same course. As pointed out in Chapter III, all scientific law arises out of observed recurrences in nature and assumes that, where there are no changes in the causal relationships, there will be no difference in the end result. We are led, therefore, to the vital question—Are there differences in our civilization that may avert a recurrence of what has taken place in the past?

Certainly our civilization is radically different from all of those that have gone before. We have developed a science and a technology that have overwhelmed the whole world. These in turn have made possible higher general standards of living than have ever been known in all human history. Although the amount of illiteracy varies widely amongst the nations of the western world, the overall level of education is clearly much higher today than in any earlier civilization. Finally, despite the steady growth of atheism, the continuing influence of the Christian tradition is still evident in the universal concern for human welfare and in the equally strong demand for individual freedom.

Although no one can foresee today just how these differences might affect the general outcome, it is conceivable that some of the factors in the current situation could change the direction in which we seem to be moving. Arnold Toynbee pinned his hopes for the future, as did Vico two centuries earlier, upon the strength of the Christian religion. Another possibility, however remote, is that a widespread awareness of the dangers that threaten our society might cause western mankind to rise up consciously and take the necessary steps to bring about a change in direction. All social laws, such as Spengler's theory of decay, presuppose a universal tendency on the part of mankind to follow unconsciously certain patterns of behavior, and such laws are operative only insofar as these conditions prevail.

This brings us to the second general conclusion that, although there is nothing logically inevitable in the doctrine of a decline of the West, the present drift in that direction appears unmistakable. A supplement to this conclusion is that, although this trend is not irreversible, any such change in the current drift will be exceedingly difficult to achieve. As noted earlier, the validity of any hypothesis is to be judged chiefly by its predictions, and the great majority of Spengler's predictions now seem to have been remarkably accurate. As a result, it is difficult to avoid the conclusion that our western culture is now in its civilization stage and has entered a period of decline.

The evidence to support this conclusion is readily available. One can see clear signs of decay in the areas of religion, politics, economics, and the arts. The one outstanding exception is found in the field of science, but even here Spengler's predictions may prove to have been premature rather than wrong. Finally, we are living today in an age of the megalopolis, with all of its frightening human, material, financial, and environmental problems. In order to present such evidence, the balance of this chapter is devoted to an examination of these several expression forms of our Faustian Culture, with particular emphasis upon the events of the past fifty years.

RELIGION

The earliest and most basic expression of the Weltanschauung of each culture is found in its religious beliefs. These early faiths provide the principal unifying factor for the development of all the other expression forms of the culture. A discussion of Spengler's treatment of the Faustian religion is, therefore, fundamental to an understanding of his predictions of a decline of our western civilization. At the outset, however, it is important to appreciate his own personal attitude toward religion.

Spengler may be described as a non-believer in the divinity of Jesus but had, nevertheless, a profound and sympathetic understanding of religious faith in all of its higher manifestations. Thus, Spengler distinguishes carefully between the teachings of Jesus, the Man, and the Christian Church which only came into being as a result of the belief in the Resurrection. In a later book, the author of the *Decline* expresses his general attitude very clearly: *"My kingdom is not of this world* is the deep saying which is true of every religion and is betrayed by every church."[1]

Spengler's treatment of the historical figure of Jesus displays a tenderness that is reminiscent of Ernest Renan's *La Vie de Jesus.* In one moving passage Spengler wrote: "The incomparable thing that lifted the infant Christianity out above all religions of this rich springtime is the figure of Jesus. In all the great creations of those years there is nothing which can be set beside it. Tame and empty all the legends and holy adventures of Mithras, Attis, and Osiris must have seemed to any man reading or listening to the still re-

---

[1]Spengler, The Hour of Decision: Knopf, New York 1936, p. 125.

cent story of Jesus's sufferings—the last journey to Jerusalem, the last anxious supper, the hours of despair in Gethsemane and the death on the cross."[2]

Spengler also saw clearly the basic antagonism between Judaism and the teachings of Jesus. All Magian peoples looked forward to the coming of a Messiah but in Jerusalem the belief was in the Messiah of their old sacred books, a Messiah who was to appear for the Jewish people and only for them. This narrow tribal exclusiveness was utterly alien to Jesus who saw that the nation of the Redeemer was identical with mankind. It was this conflict that led to the repudiation of Jesus by the Jews of Judea and to his final crucifixion.

The author of the Decline then points out that the Disciples knew little about the birth and childhood of Jesus, and that the legends which developed in this connection had not yet come into existence at the time (about 65 A.D.) of the writing of the first Gospel, that according to Mark. It is also noted that the idea of the Messiah being born of a virgin was deeply imbedded in the apocalyptic teachings of earlier Magian prophets. Spengler then observes that this myth, as adapted to the life of Jesus, had tremendous consequences for the later development of Christianity. "There presently arose beside Jesus a figure to which he was Son, which transcended his figure—that of the Mother of God. . . . But the Faustian Culture, again, when it awoke and needed a symbol whereby to express its primary feeling for infinity in time and to manifest its sense of the succession of generations, set up the *Mater Dolorosa and not the suffering* Re-

---

[2]Spengler, *The Decline of the West,* Vol. II, p. 212.

deemer as the pivot of the German-Catholic Christianity of the Gothic Age."[3]

Thus, according to Spengler, Faustian man created a new religion of his own with Mary, the Mother of God, superseding Jesus as his principal deity. Although Spengler presented this thesis definitively, others have had glimpses of the same idea. For example, George Santayana, in a beautiful passage, wrote the following:

"In northern Christianity a fresh quality of brooding tenderness prevailed over the tragic passion elsewhere characteristic of Catholic devotion. . . . The feudal ages were a wonderful seed-time in a world all gaunt with ruins. . . . Something jocund and mischievous peeped out even in the cloister; gargoyles leered from the belfry; while ivy and holly grew about the cross. The Middle Ages were the true renaissance. Their Christianity was the theme, the occasion, the excuse for their art and jollity, their curiosity and tenderness; it was a far cry from being the source of those delightful inventions. The Crusades were not inspired by the Prince of Peace, to whose honour they were fancifully and passionately dedicated; so chivalry, Gothic architecture, and scholastic philosophy were profane expressions of a self-discovering genius in a people incidently Christian."[4]

Henry Adams caught something of the same vision. In his *Mont-Saint-Michel* and *Chartres,* he contrasted the architectural styles of these two churches as reflections of the differing religious beliefs of their creators. On the one

---

[3]Spengler, *The Decline of the West,* Vol. II, p. 224.
[4]George Santayana, *The Life of Reason,* Scribner's. New York, 1922 Vol. III, pp. 112–113.

hand, the builders of Mont-Saint-Michel on the Norman coast in the 11th Century were the immediate descendants of the Norse barbarians who had invaded northwestern Gaul. Although the Normans were recent converts to Christianity, their God still remained a god of War, and their patron saint was Saint Michael, the warrior archangel. As a result, Mont-Saint-Michel[5] is more like a fortress than a Gothic cathedral. On the other hand, Notre Dame de Chartres was constructed about 150 years later during which time the religious faith of the north had undergone a radical transformation. Thus, Adams saw in the Chartres cathedral, with its delicate pointed arches and its tremendous expanse of stained glass windows, a magnificent expression of the adoration of Mary, the Mother of God.

A logical sequel to the focussing of heavenly love upon the Mary-image was the idea that earthly love is linked to the Devil, that the Devil rules only through woman, and that the witch is the propagator of deadly sin. These beliefs led to the burning of witches as a logical means of freeing doomed souls from the Devil. They led in turn to the foundation of the Inquisition. Spengler describes Inquisitors as believers who in tears and compassion, doomed heretics to the rack in order to save their souls. "That is the Gothic myth, out of which came the cathedral, the crusader, the deep and spiritual painting, the mysticism. In its shadow flowered that profound Gothic blissfulness of which today we cannot even form an idea."[6]

---

[5]Henry Adams, *Mont-Saint-Michel and Chartres,* Houghton Mifflin, New York, 1913.
[6]Spengler, *The Decline of the West,* Vol. II, p. 290.

Spengler placed great emphasis upon the value for Gothic man of the sacrament of personal contrition, which grew out of a universal longing for grace—"Not the Magian grace coming down as a substance, but the Faustian grace that unbinds the will. *To be able to will freely is,* at the very bottom, the one gift that the Faustian soul asks of heaven. . . . Every confession is an autobiography. . . . This peculiar liberation of the will is to us so necessary that the refusal of absolution drives to despair, even to destruction."[7]

The author then makes the point that since no man is capable of granting full absolution to himself the ritual of confession probably brought more happiness into the world than any institution in any other religion. In fact, with the decline of this sacrament, a sense of insecurity emerged and the Gothic blissfulness and the Mary-world of light gradually disappeared. For the Protestant and the Puritan there was no longer any joy of life; only the realm of the Devil remained with which they were forced to contend in a grim, never-ending battle. Although Puritanism does not in itself represent a decline in religious faith, it is the harbinger of the later Age of Enlightenment when atheism begins to appear. This late period development is basically an intellectual protest against the uncritical intuitiveness of the springtime. "They are enthusiasms of a sober spirit, cold intensities, dry mysticism, pedantic ecstacy. . . . Milton, Cromwell's great Secretary of State, clothed concepts with shapes, and Bunyan brings a whole mythology of concepts into ethical-allegorical activity. From that it is but a step to

---

[7]Spengler, *The Decline of the West,* Vol. II, pp. 292–4.

Kant, in whose conceptual ethics the Devil assumes his final shape as the Radically Evil."[8]

The decline in religious faith and the concurrent growth of atheism during the past two centuries have been so obvious that there is very little novel that may be said in this connection. They were already evident in the writings of Voltaire, with his famous remark about the church—"ecrasez l'infame." A full century after Voltaire this trend was noted by Matthew Arnold in the following poignant lines of verse:

> "The sea of faith
> Was once, too, at the full, and around earth's shore
> Lay like the folds of a bright girdle furled.
> But now I only hear
> Its melancholy, long withdrawing roar,
> Retreating, to the breath
> Of the night-wind, down the vast edges drear
> and naked shingles of the world."[9]

It does seem true, however, that the pace of the movement towards atheism has accelerated during the 20th Century. During the two preceding centuries the loss of religious faith was limited largely to a small group of intellectuals; philosophers, scientists, novelists, etc., while the great mass of individuals in our society remained relatively untouched. They continued to worship as their fathers had, brought their children up in church, and displayed little evidence of any loss of faith.

---

[8]Spengler, *The Decline of the West;* Vol. II, pp. 302–303.
[9]Matthew Arnold, *Dover Beach.*

An interesting contrast between the contemporary religious attitude and that of the 19th Century is provided by the public reception accorded two biographies of Jesus published just a century apart. Both are entitled *The Life of Jesus* and both treat Jesus as a natural man. The first was written by Ernest Renan in the eighteen-sixties, and the second by an Italian scholar, Marcello Craveri, published in Italy in 1966, and in the United States in translation in 1967. Renan's book, a gentle and sentimental story, was greeted throughout the Western world by a tremendous furor and outburst of indignation.[10] Craveri's book on the other hand, has caused scarcely a ripple of excitement in the United States outside of ecclestiastical circles. Much more scholarly and ruthless in its presentation of evidence to prove that Jesus was in fact a natural man, it has had widespread acceptance as probably the most authentic account yet written of the actual facts about the life of Jesus.

Even as late as the nineteen-twenties the Scopes trial in Tennessee concerning the right to teach the theory of evolution in public schools revealed a deep schism between the religious Fundamentalists and the so-called Modernists. Today, while many in small towns and rural areas still cling to Fundamentalist doctrines, the meaning of the word has almost been forgotten by the great majority of individuals in our large urban centers.

---

[10]An extraordinary example of the indignation felt by readers of Renan's book is found in the diary kept by General Charles "Chinese" Gordon during the siege of Khartoum in 1884. Surrounded by wild hordes of Mahdists and facing almost certain death, Gordon's diary shows much more concern with the infamy of the man who dared to treat the Son of God as an ordinary mortal than it does with the enemy outside the gates. The end of the story is that Khartoum was captured and Gordon slain in January 1885, just two days before the arrival of a British relief expedition.

On the surface the Protestants appear to be more affected by this trend than the Roman Catholics. Adults still flock to Protestant churches in large numbers, and their children continue to attend Sunday School. It is clear, however, that this activity has become more of a social ritual than evidence of deep religious faith. Meanwhile, increasing numbers, particularly of the affluent, either stay at home or play golf on Sundays, and use the church solely for baptisms, weddings and funerals. The Protestant clergy, frustrated in their efforts to teach a spiritual way of life to their congregations, have turned more and more in the direction of social welfare activities, civil rights problems, and any "liberal" cause that may turn up.

The rigid facade of the Roman Catholic organization has tended to conceal the appearance of any cracks beneath the surface. Nevertheless, it is evident that the Catholic Church is suffering from the same disease that is afflicting the Protestant groups. Everywhere the Church of Rome has become mainly a refuge for the poorer classes. For the middle and upper classes, particularly in the Latin and Latin-American countries, church membership has become a highly formalized activity, to be used only when it is socially expedient. The current battle within the church over the issue of birth control has served to bring these difficulties out into the open. During Holy Week of 1969, Pope Paul VI made for the first time a public admission of this situation. Speaking to a large group of Easter pilgrims in Rome, the Pope declared that the church is suffering from authoritarian regimes in many countries, from the abandonment by Catholics of their faith, and above all from criticism of its authority. "It is suffering because of the defection and scandal of certain churchmen and religious laymen, who today are crucifying the church."[11]

Probably no religious group has suffered more from the rise of atheism than the Hebrew Church. Jewish intellectuals in great numbers have become alienated from the church of their fathers and this trend appears to be continuing unabated. The Jewish faith has always been noted for its stern moral code, which has stressed the importance of sexual continence. Today, however, amongst the alienated Jews of Hollywood and Broadway, the emphasis appears to be in the opposite direction.

The only remaining religious concept to be discussed is that of "Second Religiousness." Spengler states that this phenomenon appears in the late civilization phase of every culture when it is beginning to pass into a non-historical state. He also remarks in passing that our western civilization is still many generations removed from this development. As rationalism fades out, the religious forms of the early springtime begin to emerge, and finally the whole world of the primitive religion returns to the foreground in the guise of a popular syncretism.

Meanwhile, Spengler expresses nothing but scorn for the various religious cults that have emerged during the past century in our Faustian world. In this category he includes "the occultist and theosophist fraud, the American Christian Science, the untrue Buddhism of drawing rooms—Everywhere it is just a toying with myths that no one really believes, a tasting of cults that it is hoped might fill the inner void. The real belief is always the belief in atoms and numbers, but it requires this highbrow hocus-pocus to make it

---

[11]Chicago Tribune, April 3, 1969.

95

bearable in the long run. Materialism is shallow and honest. Mock religion is shallow and dishonest."[12]

From all the above I can only conclude that we are living in an age of growing atheism throughout the western world. Is there any real hope, then, of a reversal of this trend and a revival of genuine spirituality within the near future? I am afraid my answer must be in the negative because I agree with Spengler that the real faith of the present day is in atoms and numbers. Unless, or until we lose our belief in the omnipotence of science, there can be little hope of a change in our basic attitude toward religion. Thus, I accept the view that atheism has become one of the primary facts in our western world, and that its impact will become progressively greater with the passage of the years. Religion has always provided much of the glue that holds a society together. From this it follows that the widespread loss of faith must be an important factor in the growing violence of our younger generations, and the loss of a sense of direction that is so apparent today amongst all of the nations of the West. For example, how long can the United States of America, which was founded on the firm rock of Christian faith, remain strong and united without the underpinning of these religious convictions? The basic problem of our society is, therefore, a spiritual one and may be likened to the question asked by Jesus: "What shall it profit a man if he shall gain the whole world and lose his own soul?"

POLITICS

A discussion of Spengler's political views must start with

---

[12]Spengler, *The Decline of the West*; Vol. II, p. 310.

an understanding of his concept of race. Like Nietzsche before him, Spengler was in no way a *racist* in the modern sense of the word. He was not anti-semitic, anti-negro, or an advocate of the "blond beast." For him, race meant a society that develops a common outlook on life and a unity of spirit, regardless of ethnic backgrounds. He states that the "Americans" did not migrate from Europe. Individual men migrated and they only became an American race in the true sense of the word as a result of the effect of the landscape upon their natures and, more importantly, as a result of the spiritual upheavals of the American Revolution in the 18th century and of the great Civil War ninety years later.[13]

Also fundamental to the Spenglerian philosophy is the author's distinction between the two prime estates—nobility and priesthood. Nobility (and peasantry) are plant-like and instinctive, attached to their ancestral lands, and interested primarily in the propagation of their families. The priest-

---

[13]In his epic poem, *John Brown's Body,* Stephen Benét expressed similar views as to the Americanization of the European settlers:

> "They tried to fit you with an English song
> And clip your speech into the English tale.
> But, even from the first, the words went wrong,
> The catbird pecked away the nightingale."

> "The homesick men begot high-cheekboned things
> Whose wit was whittled with a different sound
> And Thames and all the rivers of the kings
> Ran into Mississippi and were drowned."

> "They planted England with a stubborn trust
> But the cleft dust was never English dust."

JOHN BROWN'S BODY by Stephen Vincent Benét. Holt, Rinehart and Winston, Inc. Copyright, 1927, 1928 by Stephen Vincent Benét. Copyright renewed 1955, 1956 by Rosemary Carr Benét. Reprinted by permission of Brandt & Brandt.

hood, on the other hand, is the counter-estate, and with a free timeless consciousness. "Man as peasant or noble turns towards, man as priest turns away from woman. . . . For a man of race death begins to be real and appalling only when it is death without heirs. . . . But for the priest *media vita in morte sumus*: what he shall bequeath is intellectual, and rejected woman bears no part of it . . . when the priest gives up property, he is giving up something dangerous and alien: when a noble does so, he is giving up himself."[14]

Spengler makes clear that the antagonism between the two estates has been a phenomenon peculiar to our western world, and that it did not exist in the other cultures. Moreover, the struggle between these two conceptions of life has continued unabated up to the present day. The chief difference in recent times has been a change in the composition of the two groups. Thus, as the importance of the hereditary nobility has diminished, the leadership of the "fact" men has been assumed by business entrepreneurs and military leaders. Similarly, the priesthood has been pushed aside into a role of minor importance by the growing army of lay intellectuals; academicians, scientists, writers, radio and television commentators, and professional revolutionaries. Today we can see vividly the continuing polarity in the alignment in the spiritual heirs of these two antagonistic groups; the intellectual liberals on one side, and the "fact" men of the modern world on the other. Each side professes to see nothing but error in the philosophic attitude of the other, and nothing but righteousness in its own.

For the typical conservative, the intellectual liberal has become the Mephistopheles of the contemporary world, en-

---

[14]Spengler, *The Decline of the West;* Vol. II, pp. 336–343.

gaged in a conspiracy to corrupt the youth and to over-throw the so-called "Establishment." For example, James Burnham has written an entire book in an effort to authenticate this point of view.[15] Also a well-known British journalist has recently published an article entitled *The Decade of the Great Liberal Death Wish,* from which the following is quoted:

"Previous civilizations have been overthrown by the incursion of barbarian hordes; ours has dreamed up its own dissolution in the minds of its intellectual elite. It has carefully nurtured its own barbarians—all reared on the best Dr. Spock lines; sent to progressive schools and colleges, fitted with contraceptives or fed birth pills at puberty, mixing D. H. Lawrence with Coca-Cola, and imbibing the headier stuff (Marcuse, Chairman Mao, Malcolm X) in evening libations of hot chocolate. Not bolshevism, which Stalin liquidated along with all the old Bolsheviks; not nazism, which perished with Hitler in his Berlin bunker; not fascism, which was left hanging upside down, along with Mussolini and his mistress, from a lamppost—none of these, history will record was responsible for bringing down the darkness on our civilization, but liberalism. A solvent rather than a precipitate, a sedative rather than stimulant, a slough rather than a precipice; blurring the edges of truth, the definition of virtue, the shape of beauty; a cracked bell, a mist, a death wish."[16]

Despite certain elements of truth in this extreme statement, I have spent too many years in academic circles to

---

[15]James Burnham, *Suicide of the West,* Arlington House, New Rochelle, N. Y. 1964.
[16]Malcolm Muggeridge, Esquire Magazine, Dec. 1970.

swallow any such simplistic explanation. Intellectuals are individualistic to a high degree. As such, they are scarcely capable of entering into a conscious conspiracy of any kind. If they appear to be united in their attitudes it is partly because of the atmosphere in which they live and partly because of their particular cast of thought. From my own experience I am fully aware how difficult it is to live in an academic milieu and not to become imbued with the liberal philosophy. On the other hand, it is equally difficult to be part of the business world and to avoid becoming a convert to the conservative point of view.

It is true that a high percentage of the intellectuals are idealists and instinctive reformers. Such individuals tend to be overly optimistic as to their ability to solve almost any problem by the application of more democracy and egalitarianism. As a result, they are often naive and even gullible in their understanding of practical affairs outside of their own intellectual bailiwicks.*

It should be noted now, however, that the business world is perhaps equally naive in its attitude toward the intellectuals. For example, many businessmen believe that if only they could impart to the intellectuals an understanding of the *true* economics, the latter would become wholehearted supporters of free enterprise. Nothing could be further from the truth. The "fact" men in our society tend to ignore the weaknesses and abuses in our economic system which to the liberal reformers stand in such obvious need of correction.

Regardless of which side in this continuing controversy is fundamentally right or wrong, it does seem clear that the

---

* See appendix at end of this chapter for discussion of the origins and rationale of 20th century liberalism.

20th century variety of liberalism (very different in kind from 19th century liberalism which in general meant liberation rather than control) has become the dominant political philosophy of our age. This result has come about, not because of any special power wielded by the intellectuals, but rather because a majority of the politicians in the western democracies realize that the adoption of this philosophy is the surest way to win votes.

We turn now to a discussion of Spengler's theory that democracy or representative government is merely a transitional phase between the rule of an aristocratic elite and the coming of the Caesars. In this connection Spengler emphasizes the point that democracy is successful during this transitional period only in cases where an aristocracy is able to maintain a firm control of government under the outward forms of democracy. Such an example was provided by Great Britain during the 18th and 19th Centuries. Another example can be seen in the first half century of the history of the United States of America during which the reins of our national government remained in the strong hands of a land-owning elite.

A similar conclusion to that of Spengler was reached by Vico almost two centuries earlier: "In turn the popular states become corrupt. Thus they caused the commonwealths to fall from a perfect liberty into the perfect tyranny of anarchy as the unchecked liberty of the free peoples which is the worst of all tyrannies."[17] Likewise, Alexis de Tocqueville warned of the same dangers for the United States. In his famous essay, *On Democracy in America,*

---

[17]Giambattista Vico, *The New Science,* Cornell University Press, 1949.

published in 1835 after an extended visit to this country, de Tocqueville pointed out the weaknesses of a system of universal suffrage and the dangers inherent in a "spoils" system of politics.

In 1917 the United States entered a World War in order "to make the world safe for democracy." A half-century later, we can now look back and see how far short of this goal the world has fallen. Glancing first at Europe, it is chiefly in the northern countries—Great Britain, West Germany, Belgium, Holland and Scandinavia that representative government continues to function with a fair degree of success. Switzerland, of course, should be added to this group. In France and Italy it has been faltering for many years, and in Spain and Portugal it has long since disappeared. The Republic of Israel is the only nation in the eastern Mediterranean area where democracy appears to be firmly entrenced. There is, of course, no question of democracy in all the nations behind the Russian Iron Curtain.

In the rest of the world the United States, Canada, Australia and New Zealand, all of which have backgrounds of Anglo-Saxon tradition, provide the principal examples of a continuing successful operation of the system of representative government. In Latin America, with the possible exception of Mexico, democracy has become a farce. Even Mexico has lived under a one-party system of government for the past several decades. In Asia, Japan appears to be functioning satisfactorily under representative government. The permanence of democracy in India, on the other hand, remains a big question mark. Elsewhere one can see practically nothing but communist dominated countries or military dictatorships.

It may not be true that democracy is merely a transitional form of government. It remains beyond dispute, however, that true representative government can function satisfactorily only in nations where certain conditions are present. Such conditions include a strong tradition of self-government, a well-developed middle class and widespread education. Where such conditions prevail, as in the United States and Canada, democracy seems to be the most satisfactory form of government yet evolved by civilized man. For the great majority of the nations of this world, however, the only choices may be either a military dictatorship or else a Communist dictatorship.

Having declared that the United States is one of the relatively few countries in the world where conditions are favorable for a preservation of democracy, it is now pertinent to inquire as to the changes that have taken place in American democracy during the past half-century. Are these signs of deterioration, and have new dangers appeared which threaten the existence of our form of government?

Spengler stated that "the more nearly universal a franchise is, the *less* becomes the power of the electorate."[18] He also declared that universal education has weakened the power of the electorate because it has made them more subject to the power of the press. Although there are important elements of truth in both of those statements, there seems little present evidence that such developments have weakened the structure of American democracy. One indication

---

[18]Spengler, *The Decline of the West*, Vol. II, pp. 455–462.

of the stability of our national government is the fact that between 1900 and 1968 the Republican and Democratic parties have each won nine presidential elections. Another indication is that all efforts to date to create third parties have proved abortive. Walter Lippmann once wrote that democracy functions most successfully where there are no fundamental issues dividing the political parties, such as those which tore this country apart during the great Civil War.

Spengler held greatly exaggerated notions as to the power of the press. When the *Decline* was written, radio and television had not emerged as important news media; otherwise the author undoubtedly would have included them in the same category as the press. Spengler saw in news media an example of the dominance of money in the modern world, and believed that the owners of the press would control public opinion without the electorate being aware of it. The actual facts in the case, however, seem to tell a different story. For example, the magazine *Editor and Publisher* has reported that, in the 1960 election, Nixon had the editorial support of 731 leading newspapers while only 208 supported Kennedy—and yet Kennedy won. In 1968, 634 daily papers supported Nixon and only 146 favored Humphrey—and Nixon won the election by a mere eyelash.

Another surprising fact is that, with a few outstanding exceptions, the owners of the news media—radio and television stations as well as newspapers—seem to exercise little control over the views expressed by their writers and commentators. The latter are usually members of the intellectual class and many of them have political philosophies radically different from those of the owners. As a result, one frequently sees a definite cleavage between the views expressed on the editorial page and those appearing elsewhere in the newspaper. A similar situation exists in the case of radio and television, where the commentators usually give their own slant to the news, regardless of what may be the political philosophy of the owners.

Spengler constantly emphasizes the close relationship between democracy and plutocracy. "If by 'democracy' we mean the form which the Third Estate (Middle Class) as such wishes to impart to public life as a whole, it must be concluded that democracy and plutocracy are the same thing under the two aspects of wish and actuality, theory and practice, knowing and doing. It is the tragic comedy of the 'world-improvers and freedom-teachers' desperate fight against money that they are *ipso facto* assisting money to be effective. . . There is no proletarian, not even a Communist, movement that has not operated in the interest of money, in the directions indicated by money, and for the time permitted by money—and that, without the idealist amongst its leaders having the slightest suspicion of the fact."[19]

Spengler also saw in money the power that must inevitably destroy democracy. Thus, he states that, during the early years of the civilization phase of a culture, the giant cities begin to dominate the national economies and drain the vitality of the surrounding countryside. In this atmosphere democracy and money achieve their last and greatest victories. These triumphs, however, cannot last permanently because the Megalopolis inevitably destroys the old orders of the culture. In doing so it creates a chaotic situation which is the prelude to the coming of the Caesars. Confronted by this new power both money and democracy

---

[19]Spengler, *The Decline of the West,* Vol. II, pp. 401–2.

collapse simultaneously. "Through money, democracy becomes its own destroyer after money has destroyed intellect. ... Men are tired to disgust of money economy."[20]

Until recently it has been hard to reconcile such sweeping statements with the apparent stability of democracy in the United States. The money economy has raised the living standards of the trades-union members to a point where they have become a new middle class. On the other hand, the steeply graduated income and inheritance taxes have tended to lessen the great extremes of wealth and poverty.

Nevertheless, there has now appeared with alarming suddenness a new development in this highly affluent nation which can only be described as a spiritual malaise. The revolt of nego militants and of white students, aided and abetted by their intellectual leaders, displays a disaffection with the money economy and an alienation from the so-called "Establishment" that is ominous. The related problems of the negroes and of the white students are discussed in some detail later in this chapter. Here it must suffice to note that this revolt may prove to be the most serious threat to our form of government and to our whole way of life that has emerged during the past century. Finally, there is no present indication that this development is merely a passing phase of adolescent youth; instead, it has all the appearance of something that is very deep-seated and enduring.

In discussing the international aspects of politics one must take note of several important developments that have appeared since the publication of the *Decline*. These include: the invention of the nuclear and thermonuclear bombs, the population explosion throughout the world, the

---

[20]Spengler, *The Decline of the West*, Vol. II, p. 464.

emergence of the United States and Russia as the two dominating super-powers of the earth, and the growing imperialistic expansion of the Communist nations.

Taking these in the order of their listing, the development of atomic weapons has placed in the hands of mankind for the first time the ability to wipe out the entire human race. The threat of such a holocaust has hung over the entire world for the past two decades and has had a vital influence on all international relations. Meanwhile two important by-products have emerged from the present nuclear stalemate. First, it is clear that the threat of such a holocaust has been a much more important factor than the United Nations in limiting the scale and in checking the spread of the small conflicts which erupt constantly (and doubtless will continue to do so) throughout the world. In this respect, and up to this point in time, the appearance of atomic weapons has proved to be a blessing in disguise.

Second, the development of these weapons has reduced the importance of mass armies and has caused a growing dissatisfaction, at least in the Free World, with universal military service and the draft. This attitude has been particularly apparent in the United States in connection with the war in Vietnam. Even without prior knowledge of atomic weaponry Spengler predicted the trend towards smaller armies: "The place of permanent armies as we know them will gradually be taken by professional forces of volunteer war-keen soldiers; and from millions we shall revert to hundreds of thousands."[21]

The enormous growth of the world's human population during the past half-century has raised a spectre that is

---

[21]Spengler, *The Decline of the West*, Vol. II, p. 429.

haunting the mind of every serious student of international relations. Although the development of modern medicine and rising standards of living have permitted a rapid growth of population in most of the nations of the world, the problem is most acute in Asia, particularly in China and India. In this area one can see vividly the reasons for the re-emergence of the Malthusian doctrine with its frightening conclusion that the only ultimate solution of this problem is through war, famine and pestilence. This development is a cause of concern for Russia as much as for the nations of the Free World, and there can be no doubt that it has enhanced the danger of a nuclear holocaust.

Modern contraceptives have placed in our hands the technical means for a solution of this problem, and are already serving as a brake on population growth in the more advanced nations of the West. The difficulty, of course, is how to get this information across to the great uneducated masses of Asia. Clearly it has become a race against time, and so far it must be admitted that very little progress has been made in this connection.

There is, moreover, a fundamental dilemma in all efforts to control population. History teaches us that the most vigorous and progressive nations are those which have maintained high rates of population growth. Thus, Spengler points out, with justification, that the decline in population of Imperial Rome was a clear-cut indication of a loss of vitality and of the will to survive. He also notes the static population of modern France as a sign of decadence, a condition which we in the United States may be approaching.

The emergence of Russia and the United States, particularly since the end of World War II, as the two great super-powers of the world has had a profound effect on all international relationships. There has been nothing mysterious about this development and its causes have been well understood by students of economic geography. Thus, the British Empire was built on the foundation of sea-borne traffic and before the appearance of good internal transportation. The coming of the railroad, however, made possible the creation of modern Germany and the emergence of the United States as a world power. Further stimulus in this direction was provided by the automobile and the airplane. The combined effect of these changes has created the two great continental empires of Russia and the United States.

The tremendous market scope of such empires in turn has permitted the development of the most advanced mass production techniques which are beyond the economic potential of smaller nations. It is not too much to say that this technological evolution made the British Empire an anachronism. It has also placed great economic pressures on the small watertight compartments of the other nation states of Western Europe.

Ever since the end of World War II, it has been obvious to many European leaders, as well as to outside observers, that Western Europe must either unite or perish. An encouraging first step in this direction was taken with the creation of the Common Market in Continental Europe under the Treaty of Rome. Further progress, however, has seemed excruciatingly slow. It has been impeded by linguistic difficulties, ancient nationalistic rivalries and, perhaps most of all, by the personality of Charles de Gaulle, with his intransigeant emphasis upon "La Gloire de la France."

The need for the creation of a United States of Western

Europe is obvious. Such a development would create a third force between the United States of America and Russia and would contribute greatly to the peace and stability of the world. As long as this goal is not reached, Western Europe must remain impotent and in danger of being crushed, economically or militarily, between the upper and nether millstones of the U.S.S.R. and the U.S.A. Perhaps now with the removal of de Gaulle from the political arena, more rapid progress may be possible, including the likely admission of Great Britain into the Common Market. Meanwhile such events as the occupation of Czechoslovakia by the armed forces of Russia and its satellites must make European leaders painfully aware that time may be running out on them.

The imperialistic expansion of the communistic nations is the last of the items listed above which call for discussion. First, however, it should be noted that the imperialism of the white races of the West reached its culmination during the early years of the present century and, with few exceptions, came to an end after the close of the first World War. Since then the West has been engaged in a slow and reluctant withdrawal, giving up its gains under the combined pressures of the rising nationalism of former colonies and the imperialistic drive of the Communist nations.

As a result, Western imperialism during the past fifty years has been largely replaced by the expansionist push of Communism. The effects of this drive have become all too apparent—the permanent occupation by Russia of the "satellite" countries of eastern Europe, Russian activities in the Middle East, in the emerging nation states of Africa, in Cuba and throughout Latin America. China, since becoming a communist state, has joined the procession, as demonstrated by its activities in Korea, Vietnam, Indonesia and Africa. In its motivation and in the tactics employed communist imperialism differs significantly from the western imperialism of the two preceding centuries. The former is inspired by a revolutionary zeal and a religious fervor that has not been witnessed since the time of Mohammed, while the latter had as its objectives an expansion of trade and an enhancement of national prestige. The Communists have also introduced a new set of tactics which are proving very difficult to check. These include: internal subversion by local revolutionaries, infiltration by armed bands of guerillas, the supplying of arms and technical advisers, etc. All this, of course, is designed to give the impression that the uprising is strictly a civil war and not an armed invasion from the outside.

The past decade has witnessed almost countless examples of the use of such tactics—amongst the new nation states of Africa, throughout Latin America, in the Middle East, and currently in Vietnam, where the activity of the Vietcong has convinced a large proportion of the outside world that this situation is in fact a local civil war and not a military invasion from the North, aided by Russian and Chinese arms.

As Walter Lippmann has demonstrated,[22] the modern democracies have shown a fatal incapacity to maintain firm and consistent foreign policies. Thus, they tend to oscillate back and forth between periods of extreme belligerency and periods of isolationism and pacifism. Evidence to support this conclusion has been clearly apparent in the national

---

[22]Walter Lippmann, *The Public Philosophy,* Atlantic—Little Brown, Boston, 1954.

sentiment and foreign policies of the United States. During World War I we displayed an aggressive militaristic spirit. During the following two decades, however, this country moved steadily in the direction of isolationism and pacifism. World War II brought about the re-emergence of a strong belligerency which was maintained during the early years of the cold war with Russia. During the past decade, however, we have seen a drift back towards isolationism and a growing erosion of our national will to oppose communist aggression. Advocates of such policies base their stand on two principal arguments:—first, that the cold war is over and that we must do nothing that might escalate the arms race; and second, that money now spent on the military establishment is more urgently needed to solve our domestic problems.

The actual facts regarding the cold war seem to lead to a very different conclusion. Many observers, of whom I am one, believe that either we have already lost the cold war or that we are rapidly losing it. Striking evidence of this can be seen in the growing nuclear capability of Russia, her greatly increased naval power and activity in the Mediterranean and in the Indian Ocean, her limited military intervention in the Middle East, her continued activities in Cuba, and her military occupation of Czechoslovakia. Also it must not be forgotten that, since the end of World War II, wherever we have taken a firm stand against communist expansion, we have been successful—in Greece, in Turkey, in Korea, and in Formosa. Finally, we should always remember that the Soviet leaders since the time of Lenin have proclaimed openly and repeatedly their intention to dominate the world, and there is little present evidence that this ambition has been abandoned.

Two other important weaknesses in the foreign policies of the western democracies should be noted. Despite the overwhelming evidence during the past half century of the steady drift toward dictatorships throughout the world, the United States, and Great Britain to a lesser extent, still cling to the idealistic notion that all dictatorships, particularly those under military leadership, must be opposed. This attitude leads us to interfere gratuitiously in the domestic affairs of other nations. A current example is seen in the opposition by the United States to the military dictatorship in Greece. Then again how can we be so naive as to believe that we must introduce genuine representative government and free elections in a country like South Vietnam which has never known anything but dictatorships of one kind or another? We entered the war in Vietnam to oppose communist aggression in response to our SEATO treaty obligations. Now it seems that our objective is to force complete democracy upon South Vietnam even if such action should lead to a communist takeover.

Another weakness appears in the ability of racial minority groups to dictate foreign policy actions of the western democracies. One example is seen in the strong support by the United States of the Republic of Israel in its struggle with the Arab nations. Another example is shown by our attempt to enforce economic sanctions against Rhodesia because of its racial policies. Why should we consider it our duty to interfere in the domestic policies of a small south African nation, while we refrain from doing anything about the communist takeover of various Latin American countries where we have hugh economic interests at stake?

In considering the present status and future outlook of the two leading communist nations, the first point to be noted is that the recent internal chaos in China has made very difficult any intelligent speculation as to the future of this vast empire. Nevertheless, some important facts are now beginning to emerge. First, the evidence seems to indicate that the internal upheavals of the past several years have subsided and that China is now moving forward rapidly in its industrial development. Second, it is clear that China is becoming an important nuclear power, although still far behind the United States and Russia in the development of atomic weapons.

In foreign relations it is apparent that China is now much more concerned with its domestic security than in revolutionary activities throughout the world. Thus, China remains fearful of military aggression by the United States and Russia, and of the rapidly growing industrial and military power of Japan. For the near future at least the Chinese government appears anxious to remain at peace with the outside world in order to concentrate all energy upon its internal development. Thus, it is conceivable that China might become the greatest industrial and military power in the world by the end of this century.

Finally, it should be noted that the present impasse between Russia and China has, beneath the surface, very little to do with questions of ideology. Instead, the problem is fundamentally one of population and space. China with its vast population of some 750,000,000 souls sees in the huge and sparsely populated areas of Russian Siberia its only real opportunity to expand and find breathing space for its people. That Russia is fully aware of the danger in this situation is evident from the current willingness of the Russian government to reach a new series of agreements with the western powers.

The case of Russia, however, is very different from that of China. Except for its exposed frontier in Siberia, Russia occupies the most strategic position in the world today from a geophysical standpoint. In his book, *The Hour of Decision,* Spengler pointed out this fact in a passage which Adolph Hitler would have been well advised to read:

"The population of this mightiest of the earth's inland areas is unassailable from outside. Distance is a force politically and militarily, which has not yet been conquered. . . . But by the same token any idea of an offensive from the West has become senseless. It would be a thrust into empty space."[23]

When these lines were written, no one had considered the possibility that one day China might become one of the leading industrial and military powers in the world. Today, however, this possibility must be taken seriously by the Russian leaders. Because of the present relative military weakness of China there seems little near-term likelihood of a major war in this area. One or two decades hence, however, the Russo-Chinese border, which extends for some four thousand five hundred miles, could become the Achilles heel of the Russian Empire.

Ever since 1918 many outside observers, including Spengler, have believed the Bolshevist Revolution to be a passing phase and that Russia would sooner or later return to a

[23]Spengler, *The Hour of Decision*; Knopf, New York, 1936, p. 61.

more normal form of government in terms of western ideals of freedom. Looking backward from the vantage point of a half century later there seems little cause for such optimism. The government in the Kremlin is firmly entrenched both against outside aggression and internal revolt. There have, been numerous changes in leadership, and some palace revolutions, but the new leaders have always maintained the same hard-fisted methods of control. Doubtless there is discontent in Russia, but it must never be forgotten that the great mass of the Russian people have higher living standards than they had under the Czars, that they take great pride in their nation's accomplishments, and feel a deep love for Mother Russia.

Although western military imperialism has largely disappeared, the enormous power of western technology continues to change the face of the earth. The worldwide influence of our technological developments forms the main burden of the thesis set forth in W. H. McNeill's recent work, *The Rise of the West*.[24] A similar viewpoint has been expressed in a recent essay by Georgi Schischkoff.[25] The latter suggests that the leveling power of western culture may cause an elimination of all different cultures and bring about a single world culture of a western type. Both writers, however, ignore the wide difference between the dominating influence of western technology and a political domination of the world by the West. The importance of this difference becomes evident when one realizes that nearly half of the world's population today is under communist rule, and that the white races constitute only about 25 percent of the

[24]W. H. McNeill, *The Rise of the West*; Chicago Univ. Pres., 1963.
[25]Georgi Schischkoff, *Spengler Studien*, Munich, 1965.

total. In contrast to the optimistic views cited above, Spengler's prediction in *The Hour of Decision* should be recalled. Here he pointed out that the gift of advanced industrial techniques to the colored races has been caused by the rising power of the labor unions in the West, and has enabled these races to mount a world revolution of their own. As a result, he expressed the fear that the final overthrow of our western civilization would be accomplished by a combination of a class war within and a race war without.

ECONOMICS

In considering the realm of economics one must start with Spengler's very interesting distinction between the Classical idea of money and that of our Faustian world. For Classical man money consisted of physical body-units of value, such as gold coins or slaves, and wealth meant an accumulation of these physical units. Money for Western man, however, has become largely functional—the creation of money being the product of the organizing and energizing of economic life. Thus, the Faustian Culture presents a maximum of organization and the Classical a minimum: Classical man never thought of intensifying his economic life and was only interested in the tangible amount of cash he could accumulate.

"As every culture has its own mode of thinking in money, so also it has its proper money-symbol through which it brings to expression its principle of valuation in the economic field. . . . The coin as money is a purely Classical phenomenon—only possible in an environment conceived wholly on Euclidean ideas, but there creatively dominant over all economic life. Notions like income, resources, debt, capital, meant in the Classical cities something quite different from what they mean to us. They meant, not economic energy radiating from a point, but a sum of valuable objects in hand."[26]

Spengler then makes the statement that, in our Faustian Culture, thinking in money generates money. "When an organizing magnate writes down a million on paper, that million exists, for the personality as an economic centre vouches for a corresponding heightening of economic energy of his field."[27]

At first glance, the idea that a business entrepreneur can create money in this fashion appears absurd. A closer examination, however, reveals this statement to be a somewhat cryptic description of what actually takes place in the creation of deposists by commercial banks. When a successful executive obtains a loan from his bank for the expansion of his business, additional credit money comes into existence by granting him a deposit in the amount of the loan. Thus, insofar as business loans and the resulting creation of deposits are concerned, one must agree with Spengler that Faustian money is a function of the heightening of energy in the economic world.

In a further contrast between the Classical and Faustian ideas of money, Spengler refers to the use of gold coins as a fossil carried over from the Classical Culture. The developments of past half century have tended to confirm the accuracy of this statement. Gold coins have practically disappeared from circulation throughout the world, and the

---

[26]Spengler, *The Decline of the West*, Vol. II, p. 486.
[27]Ibid, Vol. II, p. 492.

function of gold has been reduced to that of serving as a monetary reserve. Now recent events indicate that this final function of gold may be eliminated by a complete demonetization of the metal. In addition, silver used in subsidiary coinage is rapidly being replaced by cheaper metals, chiefly as a result of the inflationary rise in the price of silver. Hence, one can say that the money in circulation today in the Western World is almost devoid of intrinsic value. This recent experience has also demonstrated that there is no inherent weakness in the use of cheaper materials in subsidiary coinage, provided only that the supply of such coins is maintained in a proper relationship to the demand for their use.

In reviewing the events of the past half century it is important to recall that some of the most serious economic problems of the contemporary world had not come to the surface when the *Decline* first appeared in 1918. These include: the idea of the Welfare State which only emerged as a political and economic force during the great depression of the thirties; the growth of monetary inflation throughout the Free World which followed shortly afterwards as an inevitable outgrowth of the Welfare State; and the rising power of the labor unions which also became significant during the years just prior to World War II.

It is also desirable to remember that the leading nations of the West, up until 1914, had enjoyed a full century of extraordinary financial stability. This period, which began with the establishment of the gold standard by Great Britain at the close of the Napoleonic wars, lasted almost without interruption until the outbreak of World War I. There were, of course, financial crises and panics during this century but the solvency of the leading currencies was preserved and prices remained relatively stable. Even the United States managed to survive its great Civil War without suffering a devaluation of the dollar.

This achievement was made possible largely by the strong leadership of Great Britain. It was the time of the greatest glory of the British Empire when the British navy ruled the waves, and when British seaborne trade and overseas investments brought huge returns to the mother country. In the 19th Century Britain became the acknowledged financial leader of the world and the pound sterling the cornerstone of the international gold standard. With a conservative and highly developed sense of self-discipline, the British held to a financial religion in which the First Commandment was an annual balancing of the national budget. In addition, Britain had a highly flexible economy which was very sensitive to changes in the international balance of payments. If gold flowed out, credit was promptly restricted, prices and wages fell, and the balance was quickly restored.

What a contrast this picture reveals in relation to the situation in Britain that exists today! Two world wars have drained her manhood and exhausted a large part of her foreign investments. The British Empire has virtually disappeared, and has been succeeded by the British Commonwealth of nations, and this tenuous structure in turn now shows signs of disintegration. Meanwhile the United States, with its great continental empire, has become the most powerful economic and financial nation in the world. Its huge market scope has made possible advances in industrial techniques which have made largely obsolete the British industrial organization. On top of all this Britain has become a Welfare State with all the rigidities which such a system involves. Finally, the British labor unions have become fully as powerful as those of the United States and equally unwilling to accept any control over wage rates. The result, of course, has been continuing inflation accompanied by a series of devaluations of the pound, and the end of this process does not seem to be in sight. In fact, Britain's only economic salvation appears to lie in the prospect of becoming a member of the Common Market of Continental Europe. It should be noted here that strong opposition has developed in Britain to joining this west European organization, particularly among members of the trades unions. It is all too apparent that this opposition springs from the unwillingness of British workers to face the full brunt of competition from the harder working citizens of the Common Market. It also reveals a disaffection with the money economy and the unending contest among the nations of the West to achieve ever greater gains in their gross national products.

The overwhelming economic and financial power of the United States places this country in a very different position from that of Britain. Nevertheless, the inflationary trend in our economy during the past forty years shows a good deal of similarity to the trend of events in Britain. The full-blown development of the Welfare State and the unceasing upward spiral of wage rates have combined to cause a steady erosion in the purchasing power of the dollar.

Striking evidence of what has been taking place is shown in the budgetary figures of our Federal Government. When one looks at current annual expenditures of well over $200 billions, it is difficult to recall that average Federal expenditures during the twenties amounted to only about $3 billions per year. Our Federal budget has acquired an expansionary momentum of its own that seems impossible to check. In addition to the steady flood of new programs presented to the Congress, the budget has a set of built-in rigidities that politically are very difficult to alter. These include: subsidies for agriculture and welfare, veterans' payments, foreign aid, the space program, the defense budget since the advent of the cold war with Russia and the hot war in Vietnam, and, of course, the interest on the national debt which cannot be touched without causing national bankruptcy. Also, much of the legislation now on the books has forward commitments for increased expenditures in successive future years.

The philosophic justification for the emergence of the Welfare State was the economics of Lord Keynes and his many followers. The basic theory of this group was that prosperity can only be maintained by continuous injections of purchasing power into the hands of the consuming public. In this philosophy a balanced national budget becomes more of an evil than a virtue. It proved just the kind of excuse that the politicians who wish to spend, spend and elect were looking for. The results, to say the least, have been dramatic. During the past 38 years the Federal budget has been balanced only six times. The money supply (currency plus demand deposits) has risen from $36 billions at the end of 1939 to about $200 billions today. It is not surprising, therefore, that average prices during the same period have risen by more than 180 percent.

One of the most important consequences of the American inflationary spiral has been the development of large and chronic deficits in our international balance of payments. As a result, our huge gold reserve which amounted to over $23 billions some twenty years ago has fallen to about $10 billions. Further, the amount of short-term dollar credits held by foreigners has risen to an astounding current total of more than $50 billions. For the past decade this trend has demonstrated clearly that the dollar has become progressively over-valued in international markets. Various palliatives have been attempted; these include the creation of special drawing rights on the International Monetary Fund, known popularly as "paper gold," the establishment of a two-tier market for gold, and the upward revaluation of some foreign currencies. None of these developments, however, has provided more than temporary relief, and the American Government has finally been forced to recognize the facts of life by refusing any longer to redeem dollar claims in gold. It is not too much to say that this act has sounded the death knell of the gold exchange standard established at Bretton Woods after the close of World War II.

It now remains to be seen what kind of an international monetary system can be created for the future. The basic difficulty lies not in the gold exchange standard but in the chronic inflationary trends in most of the western democracies. The fundamental cause of this situation has been the incapacity of the democratic governments to balance their national budgets. It may be stated categorically, therefore, that no satisfactory international monetary system can be created unless the competitive inflationary spirals can be checked by a willingness of the various governments to cease spending more than they take in. A second factor of almost equal importance in causing the inflationary trend has been the ability of the labor unions to raise wage rates almost at will and far in excess of any possible gains in productivity. As a result the combination of chronic deficit financing and the great power of the unions to obtain excessive wage increases has led to a steady and rapid increase in prices of all kinds.

Finally it should be noted that, under the old gold standard which collapsed during the depression of the thirties, an outflow of gold served as an automatic check upon internal inflation. The events of recent decades, however, have demonstrated that the disciplinary influence of gold is no longer sufficient to stop the inflationary trend. Now, as a result of the breakdown of the postwar gold exchange standard, nothing remains in our monetary system which can serve as a brake upon the extravagant spending habits of politicians.

Another important product of the inflationary trend has been the progressive breakdown in the international movement towards free trade. For the past three decades the United States has been in the forefront of the effort to reduce trade barriers under the successive Reciprocal Trade Acts. As the leading industrial nation of the world it has been clearly in the long-run interest of the United States to follow such a course. Dean Inge, the famous "Gloomy Dean" of St. Paul's in London, declared in one of his essays that free trade is the policy of the strong, and protectionism the policy of the weak. He then added that Great Britain had turned to free trade in her hour of greatness and back to protectionism when the sceptre had passed from her hand.

It is true that tariff duties throughout the Free World have been substantially reduced during the past thirty years.

It is equally true, however, that in recent years the proponents of protectionism have discovered a highly effective device for offsetting the relatively low levels of import duties. This is through the establishment of import quotas as a means of maintaining higher domestic prices than those that prevail in international markets. Suffering from rapidly rising wage costs, many important American industries recently have been applying heavy pressure on the Congress for relief by the establishment of import quotas on shipments from low cost producing nations. The real objective of such a policy, of course, is to maintain artificially higher prices in the United States; this in turn helps to fan the flames of inflation and thus make it more difficult for our more efficient industries to sell their products abroad. If this development should be made effective on a broad scale we could very quickly find ourselves back in the situation that prevailed in 1931 when international trade stagnated as a result of a combination of high protective tariffs and a breakdown of the international monetary system.

The statesmen of most of the western democracies, including the United States, are confronted with a terrible dilemma. How can we afford all of the social programs that seem to be so urgently needed and still avoid national bankruptcy? Certainly there is no prospect of dismantling the Welfare State under a democratic system of government. We have gone too far in this direction to reverse the process without destroying the entire governmental and social structure. Unquestionably there is room for vast improvements in the administration of the Welfare system, but beyond this we shall just have to try to live with this monstrosity we have created.

From this it follows that it has become politically impossible to stop our chronic inflation by democratic methods. A study of financial history shows us that no nation has ever emerged from such an inflationary period without undergoing a sharp economic recession, or at least a combination of deflation and currency devaluation. Any such outcome, however, can no longer be tolerated in a Welfare State. If it is impossible to stop inflation by conventional fiscal policies, the only alternative seems to be the adoption of compulsory wage and price controls. Such action is now being undertaken by the American government, together with a devaluation of our currency. It remains extremely doubtful, however, that these controls can be enforced in a democracy, except for brief periods of time, or during an all-out war. The very adoption of such methods is in itself a giant step in the direction of a police state.

The financial plight of American cities has become even more serious than that of the Federal government, and many of our great urban centers are now on the verge of bankruptcy. A leading cause of this development has been the tremendous rise in all costs of administration as a result of the inflationary spiral. Another contributing factor has been the undermining of the tax base following the mass movement of the more affluent whites to the suburbs and their replacement in the cities by the blacks. Our cities can no longer find the funds to meet their share of mounting welfare costs and the wage demands of school teachers, policemen, firemen, etc., to say nothing of their inability to finance much needed improvements in such areas as mass transportation facilities, schools, hospitals, housing and the control of air and water pollution. As a result, they turn for help to their state governments, and then to the Federal government. Since the latter can provide assistance only by means of further inflationary financing, the vicious circle becomes complete.

THE MEGALOPOLIS

One of the basic concepts of Spengler's philosophy of history is the emergence and dominance of the Megalopolis, or giant city, during the civilization phase of every culture. These great urban centers provide the stage for the culmination and final death of the culture. This process involves several phases. First, we see the rise to absolute power of money as opposed to goods, followed later by the collapse of the money economy. Concurrently, the Megalopolis begins to drain and finally to exhaust the vitality and population of the surrounding countryside by its enormous power of attraction for rural people.

Another aspect of the Megalopolis is the appearance of the Fourth Estate, generally known as the urban proletariat. According to Spengler, this Estate is the absolute of formlessness and hates every sort of form, every distinction, the orderliness of property, the orderliness of knowledge. It is, in fact, a new kind of nomadism that recognizes no past and possesses no future.

"But no wretchedness, no compulsion, not even a clear vision of the madness of this development, avails to neutralize the attractive force of these daemonic creations. . . . Long, long ago the country bore the country-town and nourished it with her best blood. Now the giant city sucks the country dry, insatiably and incessantly demanding and devouring fresh streams of men, till it wearies and dies in the midst of an uninhabited waste of country."[28]

The later stages of a civilization witness a steady decline of population. This phenomenon appears first in the world-cities and then spreads to the provincial areas. Finally only the primitive blood remains alive, which is described by Spengler as the Fellah-type.

"The born world-citizens, world pacifists, and world re-concilers, alike in the China of the 'Contending States,' in Buddhist India, in the Hellenistic age, and in the Western world today—are the spiritual leaders of fellaheen. 'Panem et circenses' is only another formula for pacificism."[29]

In considering the contemporary scene, a few statistics bring out the almost breathtaking speed with which the United States has become urbanized during the 20th Century.[30] Thus, in 1910 the farm population of 32 million accounted for more than a third of the nation's total of 92 million people. By 1950 the total number of people on farms had fallen to 23 million. By 1966 there were only 11.5 million persons living on farms, or less than 6 percent of the entire population of approximately 200 million. Looking at the problem from a somewhat different angle, it should be noted that in 1969, 70 percent of the American people, or 140 million souls, occupied one percent of the total land area. while the remaining 60 million occupied 99 percent.

In addition to the development of separate giant cities, we have witnessed the emergence of huge urbanized areas, stretching in some cases with scarcely a break for several

---

[28]Spengler, *The Decline of the West,* Vol. II, pp. 102–105.
[29]Ibid; Vol. II, p. 185.
[30]New York Times, Nov. 27, 1969.

hundred miles. The most outstanding of these is the section along the Atlantic seaboard which extends all the way from Boston to Washington. Another is the area that centers around Chicago and runs from Milwaukee on the north through Gary, Indiana at the southern tip of Lake Michigan. The bay area of San Francisco and the great sprawling area of metropolitan Los Angeles present two more examples of the same phenomenon.

The tremendous growth of suburban communities since World War I has gradually filled up the open spaces between nearby urban centers. This trend was primarily the result of the development of the railroad, the automobile and good roads which enabled business people to work in the metropolis and to live in homes far removed from the urban noise and dirt. The movement, however, has greatly accelerated in recent years as a result of the mass migration of southern Negroes to the northern cities. As the blacks have moved in, the whites in increasing numbers have moved out to the suburbs. In addition, there is now under way a substantial shift in business establishments from the heart of the cities to outlying areas in order to provide more convenient and satisfactory working conditions. A startling result of these shifts is the fact that in Washington, D. C., more than 70 percent of the population is now black. Other northern cities, such as New York and Chicago, are moving rapidly in the same direction.

The great movement from the farm to the city during this century, of which the northern migration of the Negroes has been a leading factor, has been caused primarily by the technological revolution in agriculture. The mechanization of farming has not only multiplied by many times the productivity of the individual farm worker but has also greatly increased the efficiency of large-scale farming and made practically obsolete the small one-family farm. Whereas in 1910 more than one-third of the population was needed to provide food for the American nation, now less than six percent is required to perform the same service.

An objective examination of the facts of contemporary American life leads to the inevitable conclusion that we are now living in an age of the Megalopolis, with all the problems involved in such a situation. In the urban Negroes, Puerto Ricans, and Mexicans, we have a perfect example of what Spengler called the Fourth Estate, or Mass. The rapidly mounting costs of welfare payments not only represent the modern equivalent of the Roman "Panem et Circenses" but also have become a leading contributor to the approaching insolvency of our cities.

Meanwhile the cities continue to struggle with the problems caused by the mass migration of Negro farm workers to our urban centers. One of the most difficult aspects of these problems is the fact that most of the Negroes have come to the cities totally unprepared and unconditioned to cope with life in our highly industrialized society. Despite its well-known disadvantages, life on a southern farm placed no undue strains upon the mental and emotional qualities of the Negro. Life in our great urban centers, however, is something very different. Here he finds himself tossed around like a chip of wood on an angry sea. Everywhere he meets with frustrations of one kind or another. Modern technological developments are placing a steadily increasing premium on skilled labor and decreasing the opportunities for the unskilled.

Moreover, the pressures and tensions are mounting steadily. One sees this in our schools and colleges. It is also apparent throughout our business establishments, and in the progressive mechanization of our factories. Spengler noted this phenomenon in the following passage: "In every culture the quantum of work grows bigger and bigger till at the beginning of every civilization we find an intensity of economic life, of which the tensions are even excessive and dangerous, and which it is impossible to maintain for a long period."[31]

If one wishes to understand fully the position of the Negro in our highly industralized and urbanized society, there can be no escape from an effort to come to grips with the genetic aspects of the problem. Does the American Negro suffer from racial handicaps in his efforts to find a proper place for himself in the contemporary western world? At present, there seems to be a widespread conspiracy (largely unconscious) among our intellectuals and politicians to suppress all discussion of this highly controversial subject. Nevertheless, it is important to be aware of the many scientific studies in this field that have been made during the past several decades, and the conclusions reached by some of these scholars.

An excellent compilation of such scientific evidence is set forth in a book by Nathaniel Weyl[32] published in 1960 with the title, *The Negro in American Civilization.* The principal points brought out by the author are summarized below.

---

[31]Spengler, *The Decline of the West,* Vol. II, p. 477.
[32]Nathaniel Weyl, The Negro in American Civilization; Public Affairs Press, Washington, 1960.

First Weyl notes that, between 1916 and 1960, more than 240 experimental studies have been made comparing negro and white psychometric intelligence, and in most cases every effort has been made to eliminate the influence of differences in environmental and educational backgrounds. These studies have shown consistently that the average I.Q. of the Negroes is markedly lower than that of the whites. These tests also show that the I.Q. gap between the races increases with age, and further that light skinned Negroes are considerably closer in their I.Q.'s to the whites than those with darker skins.

Other important studies, made on black natives of Equatorial Africa, bring out interesting facts regarding the development of Negro children. Quoting Mr. Weyl: "The remarkably dynamic behavior and the sociability of the very young children;" wrote Dr. Berger, "was in strong contrast to the quietness and timidity of the older children. . . . The results showed that the young African child was precocious in development when compared with European or American children of the same age. The precocity was generally lost in the third year and after that time the African children were retarded."[33]

"In the epochal study of the mental capacities, psychology and psychiatry of the African Negro which he did for the World Health Organization in 1953, Carothers expounded the biological basis for the rule that length of infancy is related to ultimate mental development as follows: 'The difficulty of early learning is mainly one of cerebral complexity, and it is the rule in all mammalian life for full

[33]Weyl, *The Negro in American Civilization*, p. 145.

132

mental structure to develop early in direct relation with cerebral simplicity.' "[34]

Finally, Weyl calls attention to the important studies, including electroencephalographic tests, which have been made on the brain structure of the African native. These studies demonstrate generally a lack of full development of the prefrontal cortex which is closely associated with reasoning power and emotional stability. Another conclusion is that the African brain is primarily auditory rather than visual. Again quoting Weyl:

"Vint drew the following major conclusion from the histological studies: 'Thus from both the average weight of the native brain and from measurements of its pre-frontal cortex, I have arrived, in this preliminary investigation, at the conclusion that the stage of cerebral development reached by the average native is that of the average European boy of between 7 and 8 years of age.' "[35]

"Connected with this auditory and tactile orientation of the African Negro mind is a tendency toward paroxysmal outbursts, uncontrolled explosions of crude emotion which rise and subside with equal suddenness and without rational cause. 'With the Negro, emotional, momentary and explosive thinking predominates,' Westermann wrote, 'dependence on excitement, on external influences and stimuli, is a characteristic sign of primitive mentality. Primitive man's energy is unstable and spasmodic.' "[36]

As a biological explanation of the brain structure of the African Negro Weyl presents the following hypothesis:

[34]Ibid; p. 147.
[35]Ibid; pp. 149-150.
[36]Ibid; pp. 154.

[handwritten margin note: is misused by ... west & this author]

[handwritten margin note: all this evidence is out of the academic mainstream and is]

"The hypothesis suggested is that in the tropics climate destroys the normal social and survival advantages of superior brain power. . . . If this is so, such races should show, on the average, less cortical development than other ethnic groups. . . . Moreover, under tropical conditions, an exceptionally active and well-developed brain may be a disadvantage in the struggle for survival because of the exorbitant demands it makes on the heart. The human brain has evolved to the point where it uses up about 25% of the oxygen which man inhales. Anthropoid apes channel only about half that proportion to their brains."[37]

All this evidence suggests that the American Negroes are members of a primitive race. If this conclusion is correct, it is obviously too much to expect that these racial characteristics could be altered substantially by a changed environment over a period of one or two centuries, except as a result of interbreeding with the whites.

Many experts in this field dispute vigorously the validity of such a conclusion, usually centering their attacks upon the relevance of the comparative I.Q. tests. Perhaps, therefore, the most significant aspects of these psychometric intelligence tests are to be found, not in the superior scoring of the whites, but rather in the fact that the gap between the races increases with age, and further that light skinned Negroes are considerably closer to the whites in their scoring than those with darker skins.

This material has been presented, not in an effort to downgrade the Negro, but in the hope of creating a fuller and more sympathetic understanding of the problems of the black farm worker who finds himself in the maelstrom of

---

[37]Ibid; pp. 164–165.

one of our northern cities. If the average full-blooded Negro suffers from certain racial handicaps, he has also demonstrated many excellent and superior qualities. Thus, the Negroes have proved themselves to be the finest athletes in the world, and in almost every branch of sports. They have also shown outstanding abilities in the arts, particularly in the fields of instrumental music, singing, dancing and the drama. In addition, the Negroes possess a deeply religious instinct which, if not completely suppressed, could assist them in finding their own self-respect.

Although the battle for formal civil rights has now been fought and largely won, at least two important handicaps still exist to the economic progress of the Negro. The first of these is the stubborn refusal of many labor unions, chiefly in the building trades, to permit Negroes to become members of their guilds. These trades require skills which most Negroes can master if given proper training; but so far our politicians have refused to come to grips with the unions on this problem. Sir Arthur Lewis, distinguished Negro educator, has declared that the labor unions are the greatest enemies of the black man.[38]

A second important handicap has been the Federal minimum wage laws. As first enacted by the Congress in 1938, the legal minimum wage was set at 25 cents per hour. Since then, successive changes in the law have increased the legal minimum up to $1.60 per hour established in 1968. As pointed out by Henry Hazlitt:

"The net result of all this has been to force up the wage-rates of unskilled labor much more than those of skilled labor. A result of this, in turn, has been that though an in-

---

[38]Sir Arthur Lewis in *University* A Princeton Quarterly (Spring 1969).

creasing shortage has developed in skilled labor, the proportion of unemployed among the unskilled, among teen-agers, females and non-whites has been growing."

"The outstanding victim has been the Negro, and particularly the Negro teen-ager. In 1952, the unemployment rate among white teen-agers and non-white teen-agers was the same—9 percent. But year by year, as the minimum wage has been jacked higher and higher, a disparity has grown and increased. In February of 1968 the unemployment rate among white teen-agers was 11.6 percent, but among non-white teen-agers it had soared to 26.6 percent."[39]

The combination of all these factors has finally resulted in the series of disastrous and bloody riots that have swept like prairie fires through most of our major cities. Although the Negro has probably injured himself and his cause by these violent outbursts, they have at least had the effect of making the white majority acutely aware of the seriousness of the problem. Another important product of these conditions has been the alarming growth of crime on the part of Negroes, particularly among the Negro youth. Thus, the felony rate of the blacks has become almost three times as great as that of the national population as a whole. Moreover, the felony rate of northern Negroes has been markedly higher than that of southern Negroes. Finally, it should be noted that the Negro crime pattern is directed primarily to violence and also to sex, liquor and drug offenses.

In many respects the Negro problem appears almost insoluble, unless the black man can learn to play a more active role in improving his own lot. Once the remaining arti-

---

[39]Henry Hazlitt, *Man vs. The Welfare State,* Arlington House, New Rochelle, New York, 1969.

ficial handicaps have been removed, the problem will rest largely, though not entirely, in the hands of the Negroes. In addition, the white majority must be willing to assist the blacks in solving their problems in many ways;—in improved education, in better job training and more job opportunities, in financial assistance for those willing and able to work and in a greater sympathetic understanding.

Nevertheless, it must be admitted that so far there has been a deplorable lack of constructive leadership on the part of the blacks. All attention has been focussed upon the problems of discrimination and segregation. Even the late revered Martin Luther King, in his campaign of non-violence, actually did as much to stir up violence as any of the so-called militants. One difficulty has been that many of the higher class Negroes have moved quietly out of the city slums to the outlying districts where generally they lead useful and self-respecting lives. This, in turn, has reduced the average quality of those who remain and has eliminated much leadership potential. Also many of those who remain in the cities have been intimidated into silence by the actions of the black militants.

The Federal courts are now going to ridiculous extremes in attempting to enforce the minutiae of desegregation. Such examples are seen in the forced busing of students from one part of a city to another, and the refusal to permit public school teachers to transfer from one school to another.

The one universal panacea now suggested by most of our politicians as a solution of the problems of the urban Negroes is a massive expenditure of money for rebuilding our cities. Because of the financial incapacity of the cities, most of this money, of course, will have to be provided by the Federal government. It may be stated categorically that any such program will prove nothing without active cooperation on the part of the Negroes. Too frequently in the past we have seen how quickly the blacks can turn an urban re-development project into a new slum.

What the Negro needs and wants is to find a new self-respect as a result of his own efforts. Obviously all remaining obstacles to his progress should be removed. Also every effort should be made to provide adequate job training and job opportunities for all who are willing and able. There will still remain, however, the problem of how to remove the criminally delinquent, including professed revolution-aries, among the Negro youth from the city streets. In a po-lice state they would be herded off into forced labor battal-ions, or worse. In a permissive society such as ours, such a solution is obviously impossible. A striking example of the difficulties inherent in this problem can be seen today in Cairo, Illinois. In this small community, already torn by years of racial strife, a group of conservative, high-grade Negroes is contending for leadership of the black popula-tion with another group of revolutionary militants. If the former group wins, we might see the emergence of a pattern which could bring racial peace to our cities. If, however, the revolutionaries are successful and can spread their success to other communities, we may find ourselves on the verge of a civil war.

Complete social integration of the two races is a Utopian dream, at least for the forseeable future. Already this ideal is proving as unenforceable as Prohibition. The whites sim-ply will not accept it, and the blacks, when they attain it, suddenly discover that they dislike it also. Some revealing examples of this phenomenon have appeared in the attempts to integrate college dormitories. Almost immediately after reaching this objective, the black students have reversed their position and demanded separate dormitories for members of their own race.

Finally, it should be stated that considerably more time may be needed before we find a satisfactory solution of the Negro problem. The position of the blacks in our society has been vastly improved during the past two decades and further progress in this direction appears likely. If the blacks are able to develop a strong law-abiding leadership, the problems created by the militant and revolutionary members of their race can be brought under control. If, however, they fail to do so, the present cancerous sore in the heart of our body politic can only widen and deepen until it becomes an important contributing factor in the decay of our civilization.

Another frightening development of our urbanized society is the threatened breakdown of our educational system. In considering this problem two separate phases should be noted. The first covered the two decades between 1946 and 1966, and the second has become evident only during the past four to five years.

During the first phase, returning veterans, rising standards of living and population growth placed great pressures upon the physical and intellectual facilities of all our institutions of higher learning. This development reached its peak during the early Sixties when the wave of the immediate postwar "baby boom" hit the secondary schools and colleges. For most of the private institutions this huge influx of students caused a progressive rise in entrance requirements and enhanced the pressure of work after a student had been admitted. For many of the public high schools and state universities, however, the desire of the authorities to provide higher education for all applicants has resulted in an actual lowering of scholastic requirements, particularly in the case of Negroes.

The second phase began to appear in middle Sixties. It has been caused by rapidly rising costs combined with a decline in the student population. Although all of our institutions of learning are suffering from the inflationary spiral of rising costs the chief impact of this development has fallen on the private schools and colleges. During the past few years Catholic parochial schools have been closing in large numbers and most of the Protestant and non-denominational institutions are now engaged in a desperate struggle for survival. In addition to an actual decline in the student population, the private schools and colleges have been forced to raise tuition costs to a point where it is driving large numbers into public institutions of learning.

This problem has been greatly aggravated by the contemporary revolt of college students. A discussion of this situation must start with the statement of a few basic facts. First, although the problem has been accentuated in the United States by the war in Vietnam, the current revolt is not just an American phenomenon, but is widespread throughout the Free World. The second is that it is not just a problem of the black students or of the whites, but the two are so intermingled that it is not possible to separate them. Finally, it seems clear that this development is not basically a communist revolt. Although there are strong communist elements involved, the movement appears to be more in the nature of a nihilistic rebellion against all authority and discipline. Thus, it represents a growing alienation from our society and a strong dislike of the money economy. In fact, it may be described as a modern version of "a burning of the books."

Although the causes underlying this phenomenon are highly complex and defy any simple analysis, some factors stand out clearly. First, it is evident that a considerable proportion of the students now in college have no genuine interest in higher education. Many are there in order to escape the military draft. Others are in attendance solely because of the belief that a college degree is necessary for later success in life. Many of the latter group, chiefly in the public institutions of learning, have arrived at the college level without adequate training in the fundamental disciplines of reading, writing and mathematics. Others simply do not possess the mental equipment to cope with a college education. All such groups are bored by the curriculum and feel a lack of relevance in the courses they are required to take. As a result, they give vent to their frustrations by lashing out blindly against the college authorities and the whole present structure of society.

Another factor of importance has been the teaching of radical doctrines by left-wing elements of the college faculties. In many cases such teachers have actually encouraged rioting and have led students to believe that they have an inherent right to break laws that they do not believe in. Added to this has been the excessive timidity on the part of college administrators in enforcing discipline. The latter have never had to cope with problems like these, and they tend to justify their permissiveness by stretching the ideal of academic freedom to ridiculous extremes. In the case of private schools and colleges an important result of these developments has been to alienate a high proportion of the alumni and friends who in the past have provided much of the financial support of these institutions.

In brief, what we seem to be witnessing is the gradual elimination of privately supported education in the United States. Without the leavening influence of these schools and colleges scholastic standards throughout the nation will inevitably be lowered and our whole structure of higher education seriously impaired.

It is important now to note that even among the peaceful and well behaved elements of the student bodies there is evidence of a growing dislike of the money economy and of the rising tensions within the social and economic organization of society. A high degree of idealism is found in the ranks of such students and many are struggling to find a greater significance in life than they can discover in what they describe as the "Rat Race" of contemporary business careers. Thus, there is a widespread sense of frustration among the youth of today, in the ranks of the orderly as well as in those of the activist rebels. There is also evident a correlation between such frustrations and the alarming growth in the use of drugs by our young men and women, as well as in the readiness with which they succumb to the radical doctrines of their teachers.

Finally, it must be admitted that there are important elements of rationality in the current revolt of the youth of our western democracies. Thus, many of our young men and women, as well as their intellectual leaders, believe that there are no longer any genuine moral values in modern industrial society, and that the only remaining goal has become that of producing an ever mounting volume of goods and services. Both business and government have become obsessed with the idea that the only road to salvation lies in an unending rise in the Gross National Product.

Business is driven in this direction in order to maintain profits in the face of steadily mounting costs. Our national governments pursue the same goal in an effort to maintain full employment. This situation is a basic cause of the steadily mounting pressures and tensions in our society, and also of the progressive alienation of our youth. Paradoxically, as a nation increases in affluence it seems evident that its problem of alienation becomes more serious. Another paradox lies in the fact that as national productivity increases as a result of advanced technology the employment problem of the unskilled is likely to become progressively more difficult. Unfortunately, there does not appear to be any avenue of escape from this treadmill, at least under a democratic system of government.

From all the above the evidence seems overwhelming that powerful divisive forces are at work today in the United States that threaten to tear the country apart. Thus, we see the wide polarity between the intellectual elite and the men of business, the racial strife between blacks and whites, and the growing alienation of the youth of all races. How we can restore a sense of national unity in the face of such influences should be a matter of grave concern. Moreover, it is equally clear that many of the problems of our western democracies are beyond the capacity of the national governments to handle. These include: chronic inflation, the power of the labor unions, and the revolt of the black militants and of the white students.

MATHEMATICS AND PHYSICAL SCIENCE

The opening chapter of the *Decline,* "The Meaning of Numbers," is one of the most interesting and provocative sections of the entire work. It is a startling experience for most readers to realize that an apparently simple concept like "number" could have had such radically different meanings for the peoples of the several High Cultures. The simple, visible space mathematics of Euclid is followed by the algebra of the Magian world. With its unknown, indefinite and negative numbers, it had a magical quality about it; it would have been incomprehensible to Classical man who could think only in terms of positive, concrete numbers.

Algebra in turn was succeeded by the mathematics of the Faustian Culture. Here we see a development that is alien to the Classical or Arabian concepts. The creation of the calculus, the mathematics of motion, the emergence of the idea of functional analysis, or of relations between magnitudes, and finally the development of the non-Euclidean geometries and the theory of relativity all exemplify the unique character of our western mathematics.

The Faustian Culture also removed Euclidean geometry from its pedestal. To the layman, Euclidean geometry seems to be (and always has seemed to be) the only true and valid geometry. This in spite of the fact that the evidence of the senses actually tells us that parallel lines meet (think of parallel railroad tracks). Mathematicians, from Gauss' time on, have known that Euclid's axiom of parallels—the cornerstone of his geometry—cannot be proved or disproved. It is in fact nothing but a hypothesis and as such no more valid than any other consistent hypothesis.

Applied mathematics is always the handmaiden of physical science and both mathematics and physics tend to develop cojointly. Experimental science emerged in the Faustian world in the 16th and 17th Centuries and, as it progressed, technology became steadily more important. The intimate relationship between mathematics, physical science and technology in the Faustian Culture is the characteristic that has made it unique in all human history. Thus, Spengler notes that the view that "knowledge is virtue" is common to many cultures. Confucius believed it, and so did Buddha, as well as Socrates. But the phrase that "knowledge is power" possesses meaning only within the European-American civilization.[40]

"Within Baroque philosophy western natural-science stands by itself. No other culture possesses anything like it, and assuredly it must have been from its beginnings, not a "handmaid of theology," but *the servant of the technical will-to-power,* oriented to that end both mathematically and experimentally—from its very foundations a practical mechanics. . . . For us the first thing is ever the working hypothesis—the very kind of thought-product that is meaningless to other cultures."[41]

Spengler illustrates the importance of the working hypothesis in Faustian nature knowledge by means of potential and field theory, notions which according to him would have been impossible for Classical thought. All the impor-

---

[40]Spengler, *The Decline of the West,* Vol. II, p. 339.
[41]Ibid; Vol. II, pp. 300–301.

tant concepts of Western science, such as "atomic theory," "magnetism," "electricity," "radiant energy," "radioactivity," and others are working hypotheses. They do not arise out of experimentation, but define the structure of nature *a priori*. Thus they are more than hypotheses; they are really *myths*. And myths, in turn, imply religious faith.[42]

"It follows then that all 'knowing' of nature, even the exactest, is based on a religious faith.[43] The pure mechanics that the physicist has set before himself as the end-form to which it is his task (and the purpose of all this imagination machinery) to reduce nature, presupposes a dogma— namely, the religious world-picture of the Gothic centuries."

According to Spengler, mathematical thought of our western world reached its culmination in the 19th Century with the non-Euclidean geometries of Gauss and Riemann, and the emergence of the idea of multi-dimensional space, which in turn produced the theory of relativity.

"And with this culmination our western mathematic, having exhausted every inward possibility and fulfilled its destiny as the *copy and purest expression of the idea of the Faustian soul,* closes its development in the same way as the mathematic of the Classical Culture concluded in the third century. . . . It is enough for the moment that for us the time of the great mathematicians is past."[44]

Although this dogmatic assertion by the author of the *Decline* was undoubtedly inspired by his effort to round out his neat pattern of cultural life cycles with the disappearance of creativity during the transition of a culture to a civi-

[42]Spengler, *The Decline of the West,* Vol. I, pp. 387, 412.
[43]Ibid; Vol. I, p. 380.
[44]Ibid; Vol. I, p. 90.

lization, the passage of a half century has demonstrated the invalidity of any such conclusion. Spengler was fully conversant with the general theory of relativity and must have been aware of Albert Einstein whose works in this field were first published in Germany in 1912 and 1916, but the latter's name is never mentioned in the *Decline*. It is true, of course, that the full impact of the Einsteinian concepts was not felt until the nineteen-twenties when evidence of the curvature of light provided experimental verification of these theories. It was then realized that Einstein in a series of sweeping generalizations had eliminated the Newtonian theories of gravitation, mass and extension. His achievement was hailed as the greatest intellectual synthesis in human history, and it was widely believed that this work did represent the ultimate in mathematical thought.

Nevertheless, various leaders in the field of astrophysics are now raising serious questions as to the universal applicability of Einstein's theories. It will be recalled that Einstein had attempted to eliminate gravitation as a field of force by his use of Riemannian geometry as a more satisfactory description of the curvature of space. Now, however, contemporary scientists are finding increasing difficulties in explaining certain experimental observations without the reintroduction of a modified theory of gravitation.[45] Although no new synthesis has yet appeared, such work in this field provides convincing evidence of the continuing vitality of scientific thought.

Spengler also believed that he saw evidence of a disintegration of physics in various developments which occurred

---

[45]cf. article by Professor Robert H. Dicke of Princeton University, *Gravitational Theory and Observation*, in "Physics Today", January 1967.

during the 19th and early 20th Centuries. First, he cites the second law of thermodynamics, otherwise known as the theory of entropy. The first law is that of the conservation of energy which in its simplest form, postulates that when heat energy is transformed into any other kind of energy, or vice versa, the quantity of energy that disappears in one form is exactly equivalent to the quantity produced in the other form. Thus, the first law is independent of time as duration and the physical processes described therein are reversible and measureable.

The second law, however, is something very different and is, in effect, a kind of amendment to the first law. Essentially, it expresses the fact that all physical changes have a tendency to be degraded into heat, and that heat tends to be distributed among bodies in a uniform manner. A simple example is seen in the slowing down of the motion of a pendulum, the energy of which is gradually transformed into heat caused by friction. The vital point in this process is that the heat so generated cannot be reconverted into energy without the application of additional work. Both Spengler and Bergson saw in the irreversible nature of entropy a break in the universal validity of scientific law, and merely a statement, in terms of historical time, of the direction in which the world is going.

Second, Spengler saw in the trend towards unification of the separate sciences—physics, chemistry, mathematics, astronomy, etc.—further evidence that Faustian science had reached its culmination and had begun to disintegrate. He expressed these ideas as follows:[45]

"Even a century ago, physics and chemistry were foreign to one another, but today they cannot be handled separately

—witness spectrum analysis, radioactivity, radiation of heat. . . . The last discussions of epistemology are now uniting with those of higher analysis and theoretical physics to occupy an almost inaccessible domain, the domain to which, for example, the theory of relativity belongs or ought to belong. The sign-language in which the emanation-theory of radioactivity expresses itself is completely de-sensualized. . . . Through the emanation of radiant energy degradation is always going on, so that we can speak of the *life-time* of an element, in formal contradiction with the original concept of the element and the spirit of modern chemistry as created by Lavoisier. All of these tendencies are bringing the ideas of chemistry very close to the theory of entropy, with its suggestive opposition of causality and destiny, nature and history. And they indicate the paths that our science is pursuing—on the one hand, towards the discovery that its logical and numerical results are identical with the structure of the reason itself, and, on the other, towards the revelation that the whole theory which clothes these numbers merely represents the symbolic expression of Faustian life."

Further evidence of this trend is found by Spengler in the quantum theory of atomic energy developed by Max Planck and Niels Bohr in the early years of the present century. The model of the atom, as originally conceived by Rutherford, consisted of negatively charged electrons revolving in orbits around a positively charged nucleus. Although winning almost universal acceptance, this theory had one flaw that puzzled scientists. Thus, they discovered that the emanation of energy did not appear in a continuous flow

---

[46]Spengler, *The Decline of the West*; Vol. I, p. 426.

but came instead in discrete packets or quanta of energy. The problem was finally solved by Planck and Bohr in their theory that electrons have not one but several different orbits in which they can revolve about the nucleus. As a result, energy is radiated from an atom only when an electron shifts from one specified orbit to another.

Spengler realized that the quantum theory of the discontinuity of energy had destroyed the Newtonian concepts of constant mass and force. He saw also in the experiments of Michelson on the velocity of light the elimination of the idea of absolute time. Spengler, therefore, concluded:— "Absolute measures of length and rigid bodies are no more. And with this the possibility of absolute quantitative delimitations and therefore the "Classical" concept of mass as the constant ratio between force and acceleration fell to the ground just after the quantum of action, a product of energy and time, had been set up as a new constant."[47]

Spengler had described Nietzsche, in his approach to the cyclical theory of history, as one who "got as far as the door —and stood outside it." A similar observation may be made about Spengler in connection with the intellectual synthesis achieved by Einstein. The former saw disintegration while the latter saw a magnificent new unification of time and space.

The only possible conclusion from the above is that the author of the *Decline* produced no convincing evidence that Faustian mathematics and physics had reached and passed their intellectual peaks. True, old theories were being discarded as experimental evidence proved them inadequate to describe observed phenomena. Even the vast panorama

[47]Spengler, *The Decline of the West;* Vol. I, p. 419.

painted by Einstein shows cracks on its surface. One can see no compelling reason, therefore, why new intellectual syntheses may not appear in the future to replace those now universally accepted.

Whereas Spengler was clearly wrong in his predictions as to the prospects for scientific thought, he was more right than he could have imagined in his prediction that one of the greatest tasks for the future of western civilization lay in the practical applications of physics and chemistry. The past half-century has been a truly fantastic period for the growth of technical developments in the various fields of physical science. Moreover, the rate of growth in these areas at present appears to be accelerating rather than diminishing. The vast sums of money currently applied to research and development by industry, charitable foundations and governmental bodies have provided a momentum that is almost breathtaking.

Examples of these developments are almost myriad, but the citation of only a few should serve to emphasize the point. Thus, we have witnessed the creation of the atomic and thermonuclear bombs out of pure theoretical reasoning of scientists, and the harnessing of atomic power for the generation of energy. Although the technical obstacles are very great, contemporary scientists are hopeful that eventually they will succeed in a similar harnessing of thermonuclear power.

Other startling developments have occurred in the whole field of electronics. The invention of television is a perfect example of the working out of technological problems in order to achieve a preconceived goal. The miniaturization of electronic components has produced a host of new controls which have tended to revolutionize industry, communications, air travel, space flight, military technology, etc. These developments in turn have made possible the evolution of the modern computer which has become so important in contemporary society that the present may well be known as the Computer Age.

Similar fantastic developments have taken place in the field of chemistry. The creation of a host of new materials—new metals, a wide variety of new plastics, and other new synthetic materials—has had a tremendous impact upon modern industry. These developments, including also the creation of modern fertilizers, pesticides, herbicides, etc., have produced a virtual revolution in agriculture as well as in industry.

The discovery of antibiotics and other "wonder" drugs, including oral contraceptives, the isolation of viruses, with accompanying development of vaccines and vastly improved surgical techniques have had far-reaching effects on medical science. These developments have not only caused a substantial prolongation of the average human life but have also made possible a solution of the population problem.

Finally, the combined efforts of physics and chemistry have introduced our society to the so-called Space Age. First came the intercontinental ballistic missiles; next, following Sputnik, the space orbiting vehicles; and then the break through into outer space. In a passage of great visionary insight Spengler foresaw these developments and described them as a perfect exemplification of the Faustian spirit with its insatiable urge to explore the infinitely far and great as well as the infinitely small.

"And what now develops, in the space of hardly a century, is a drama of such greatness that the men of a future culture, with other soul and other passions, will hardly be able to resist the conviction that 'in those days' nature herself was tottering. . . . This is the outward- and upward-straining life-feeling—true descendant, therefore, of the Gothic—as expressed in Goethe's Faust monologue when the steam-engine was yet young. The intoxicated soul wills to fly above space and time. An ineffable longing tempts him to indefinable horizons. Man would free himself from the earth, rise into the infinite, leave the bonds of the body, and circle in the universe of space amongst the stars."[48]

But the tremendous growth of science has attendant dangers. First, Spengler points out that Western science has always been esoteric in contrast to the popular and widely understood science of the Classical culture. This condition has prevailed in the arts as well as in the sciences:

"Every high creator in Western history has in reality aimed, from first to last, at something which only the few could comprehend. . . Consider our sciences too. Every one of them, without exception, has besides its elementary groundwork certain "higher" regions that are inaccessible to the layman—symbols, these also, of our will-to-infinity and directional energy. The public for whom the last chapters of up-to-date physics have been written numbers at the utmost a thousand persons, and certain problems of modern mathematics are accessible only to a much smaller circle still—."[49]

Spengler concludes the second volume of the Decline

---

[48] Spengler, *The Decline of the West,* Vol. II, p. 503.
[49] Ibid; Vol. I, pp. 327–329.

with a warning against the danger of having the entire future of our civilization rest on the shoulders of such a small number of individuals. He points out that the very existence of modern industry depends not only upon the scientists and entrepreneurs, but more importantly upon one hundred thousand highly trained technicians and engineers. "The quiet engineer it is who is the machine's master and destiny. . . . There have been fears, thoroughly materialistic fears, of the exhaustion of the coalfields. But so long as there are worthy technical pathfinders, dangers of this sort have no existence: when, and only when, the crop of recruits for this army fails—this army whose thought-work forms one unit with the work of the machine—the industry must flicker out in spite of all that managerial energy and workers can do."[50]

Next, it must be noted that physical scientists are now suffering from the mounting pressures and tensions of the modern world. The conventional idea of the scientist working alone in his ivory tower bears little relationship to presentday actualities. Scientific research has become increasingly organized until the contemporary scientist usually finds himself more of a cog in a vast machine than an isolated individual directing his own destiny.

This situation is seen most clearly in the field of high-energy physics. Here the tremendous costs of constructing, maintaining and operating the giant accelerators have forced a regimentation of the scientists involved that would have been unthinkable a half-century ago. These economic costs, which include the employment of thousands of

[50]Spengler, *The Decline of the West,* Vol. II, p. 505.

workers at each major installation, have led to the necessity of operating the huge machines around the clock. Instead of working as a separate individual, each nuclear scientist now finds himself compelled to function as a member of a team which must compete with other teams for an allotment of time to carry out their chosen experiments. In order to make maximum use of their time quota each team is placed under extreme pressure to organize its work weeks, and even months, in advance. Since a team may be composed of anywhere from a dozen to as many as fifty nuclear scientists, the result has been to reduce individual initiative, and to make very difficult the determination as to which of the scientists involved are to be given the primary credit for carrying out a successful experiment.

Whether or not scientific thought can maintain its spontaneity and dynamism under such conditions is becoming a serious question. There also remains the more fundamental question of whether our nuclear scientists in their demands for ever larger and more powerful accelerators in the effort to determine the ultimate nature of matter, understand any longer the direction in which they are moving, or whether they are pursuing a will-o-the-wisp that must forever elude them. If the latter surmise should prove correct, these scientists may find themselves in a position similar to that of the medieval scholastics who reached a *reductio ad absurdam* in their reasoning when they debated the famous problem: "How many angels can dance on the head of a pin?"[51]

---

[51]Contemporary historians now generally regard this question as a later burlesque of scholastic philosophy rather than as an actual problem debated by the scholastics. Even as a burlesque, however, it still serves as an excellent symbol of the ultimate futility of scholastic philosophy.

THE ARTS

Although one of Spengler's greatest achievements was his recognition that the various art forms have profound significance as symbols of the Weltanschauung of each culture, it is obviously impossible to cover adequately this vast and complex field within a few pages. Another important difficulty is that there are no objective criteria on which to base judgments with regard to the arts. All opinions as to artistic achievements lie chiefly in the eye of the viewer or in the ear of the listener and no one can prove that another person's judgments are right or wrong. About all that can be attempted herein is to trace the salient features of Spengler's theories of the development and decay of the arts in the Faustian world and then to arrive at a few tentative conclusions as to the state of contemporary art.

Spengler regarded architecture as the basic art of each culture and saw in the various religious edifices prime symbols of the spiritual attitudes of the men who created them. Thus, the Doric temple is all exterior; the Arabian mosque, with its cavern-like feeling, is all interior; the Gothic cathedral, with its upward thrusting vaults and its vast expanse of painted glass windows is a perfect expression of the Faustian feeling of reaching out into infinite space. Spengler also describes the Gothic cathedral style as unique in all history. Also, unique is the Gothic art of stained glass windows with its polychrome, translucent and, therefore, bodiless painting. "It is perhaps in the Sainte-Chapelle in Paris that this emancipation from bodiliness is most evident. Here the stone practically disappears in the gleam of the glass."[52]

---

[52]Spengler, *The Decline of the West;* Vol. I, p. 199.

One of Spengler's fundamental concepts is the contrast between the nude statue of Classical man from which all individual characterization is deliberately avoided, and Faustian portrait painting which is wholly biographical, the life history of an individual expressed in a moment of time. He points out, however, that, while Gothic architecture developed freely as a true expression of the Faustian spirit, western religious painting remained for several centuries under the influence of the Magian tradition with its use of the gold background. Thus, it was not until the 13th century, with the work of Cimabue and Giotto, that the gold background began to disappear and a naturalistic spirit appeared in western painting. Spengler points out that the appearance of depth perspective, blue-green heavens and far horizons coincided with the emergence of the true Faustian religious spirit; the conception of the dynamic infiniteness of God.

These developments led directly to the Italian Renaissance of the 15th and 16th centuries which Spengler describes as a brief and abortive revolt in sun-drenched Italy against the dark and brooding spirit of the Gothic north. Thus, he asserts that the Renaissance architects, painters and sculptors never came close to the true Classical spirit. Spengler points out that the models which Renaissance architects attempted to copy were not those of the great days of Hellas but those of the late Roman Empire, when the true Classical style had vanished and had been replaced by Magian models (i.e., the association of the round arch and column) which originated in Syria. He also notes that of the two famous Classical buildings of the Renaissance, the domed cathedral of Florence is in fact a masterpiece of the late Gothic and St. Peter's is one of early Baroque.

In painting and sculpture Spengler describes Michelangelo and Raphael as the chief exemplars of the revolt against the Gothic spirit. He maintains, however, that Leonardo was not part of the Renaissance revolt. Thus, he contrasts the work of Raphael and Leonardo by stating that the former displays in every brush stroke the plastic quality of his painting. Leonardo, on the other hand, is described as the first Impressionist who in his red-chalk drawings reveals aerial secrets in every line.

Michelangelo, according to Spengler, was basically a sculptor who strove to be a portrait painter. This characteristic comes out clearly in the plastic quality of his painting. Nevertheless, there was little of the Classical spirit in either his sculpture or his painting. Both were biographical and, therefore, Faustian in spirit. With the end of the Renaissance, sculpture disappears as a great art of the West because its intractable material could not express the Faustian spirit in a manner comparable with oil-painting and instrumental music. "This art had fallen out of the destiny of the Culture. Its speech meant nothing now. What there is in a Rembrandt portrait simply cannot be rendered in a bust."[53]

In his treatment of the Renaissance, Spengler brings out the important truth that no culture can ever turn its back completely on its own fundamental traditions. It may adopt forms and styles from other cultures but will alter them to fit in with its own Weltanschauung. In stressing this point, however, Spengler greatly underestimates the importance of the Renaissance in the whole development of Faustian art and architecture. Perhaps Spengler's difficulty was largely a

---

[53]Spengler, *The Decline of the West;* Vol. I, p. 244.

matter of semantics since the word "Renaissance" is now generally regarded as something of a misnomer. Thus, later historians take the position that the 15th and 16th centuries in Italy did not represent a "rebirth" of anything but that this period was, in fact, the early dawn of the modern world, in which a devotion to antiquities played a relatively minor part.[54]

Now Spengler introduces a novel idea to explain the Baroque and Rococo styles which developed out of the Renaissance between the 16th and 18th centuries. This concept is that each culture has a dominant art form which best expresses its world outlook and that this dominant art tends to influence the development of the other arts. In the Classical Culture the dominant art form was the nude statue and all the other great arts—vase-painting, fresco relief, the Doric temple, the drama and the dance—fall under the influence of this prime symbol. In the Faustian world, on the other hand, the prime symbol is pure spatial infinity, and instrumental music, which is the most complete expression of this world attitude, had an important influence on the other great arts.

Spengler contends that instrumental music, in its great development between the 16th and 18th centuries, not only freed itself from all relics of bodiliness but also tended to dominate the other art forms, particularly architecture and painting. Thus, he saw in the evolution of the Baroque style to its culmination in the 18th century Rococo a progressive effort to express music in stone.

Spengler waxes eloquent in his defense of the Rococo

---

[54]cf. J. Huizinga, *The Waning of the Middle Ages;* Arnold, London 1924.

style which he saw as representing the end term and final death of western architecture. He maintains that critics have failed to understand that the origin of this style is in the spirit of the fugue—a victory of tones and melodies over lines and walls. "They are no longer buildings, these abbeys and castles and churches with their flowing facades and porches and "gingerbread' courts and their splendid staircases, galleries, salons and cabinets: they are sonatas, minuets, madrigals in stone."[55]

At the same time he saw the growing influence of music upon painting. He describes Titian as one of the first in whose work this influence appears. In contrast to the paintings of Raphael in which is seen the plastic spirit that one associates with relief, the musical spirit of Titian is evident in his technique of visible brush strokes and atmospheric depth-effects.

Hence it is in the 16th century that a decisive change occurs in western painting with the Impressionism of Leonardo and Giorgione and the musical spirit of Titian. Colors become tones and painting becomes polyphonic, picturesque and infinity-seeking. "It is in the horizon then, that music triumphs over plastic, the passion of extension over its substance. It is not too much to say that no picture by Rembrandt has a foreground at all."[56]

The work of Rembrandt, in Spengler's view, marked the culmination of western painting, and he regarded the latter's use of the "studio brown" as a symbol of great significance. This brown is not different from the earlier blues and

---

[55]Spengler, *The Decline of the West;* Vol. I, p. 289.
[56]Ibid; Vol. I, p. 239.

greens; it is merely more powerful than they in dissolving the world of movements and foregrounds into atmospheric semblances. As such it marks the ultimate in depth-perspective and infinity-seeking of Faustian painting.

In Faustian music the human voice was the dominant factor throughout the middle ages and instrumental music served chiefly to accompany singing. Until the 16th century the Church of Rome also rejected sternly all efforts to introduce polyphonic music into its services. Spengler states that the empire of the human voice came to an end in the *a cappella* style of Palestrina and Orlando Lasso, and was superseded by the chorus of instruments, wind and string.

Out of the early forms in the Baroque period there evolved in the 17th century the immensely dynamic and bodiless forms of the suite, symphony and concerto grosso, chiefly through the work of Corelli, Handel and Bach. The final step in this development, according to Spengler, was the appearance in the 18th century of the new sonata form for stringed instruments. This change brought music from the more static form of the fugue which is essentially a picture to the more dynamic form of the sonata for strings which becomes a moving drama. "Certain it is that the violin is the noblest of all instruments that the Faustian soul has imagined and trained for the expression of its lost secrets, and certain it is too, that it is in string quartets and violin sonatas that it has experienced its most transcendent and most holy moments of full illumination . . . when one of those yearning violin-melodies wanders through the space expanded around it by the orchestration of Tartini or Nardini, Haydn, Mozart or Beethoven, we know ourselves in the presence of an art besides which that of the Acropolis is alone worthy to be set."[57]

Having reached its culmination in the 18th and early 19th centuries with the work of Mozart and Beethoven, Faustian music, in Spengler's opinion, began to show signs of decay. Spengler saw in the work of Wagner the decisive turning point in this development. In fact, he had a profound admiration for the earlier music of Wagner. At one point he refers to the latter as "that last product of the German spirit over which greatness broods." He also wrote "The last of the Faustian arts died in *Tristan*. This work is the giant keystone of western music."[58] It was Wagner's later works, specifically the *Ring* and *Parsifal* which Spengler rejected as examples of decadence and theatricalness.

After the middle of the 19th century Spengler saw nothing but decadence in the principal art forms of the Faustian world. Western architecture died with the end of the Rococo style in the 18th century. Painting and sculpture entered a period of decline with the emergence of the French Impressionist school during the latter half of the 19th century. Music suffered a similar fate after the early works of Wagner. In a series of sweeping generalizations, and with little supporting evidence, Spengler condemns all the western art of the past century as "impotence and falsehood." It is obviously impossible to accept such broad generalizations. Instead, the attempt must be made to trace the major developments in the western arts during the past century before reaching a few tentative conclusions.

First, it must be admitted that the 19th century witnessed

[57]Spengler, *The Decline of the West;* Vol. I, p. 231.
[58]Ibid; Vol. I, p. 291.

a shocking deterioration in architectural taste. In the field of domestic architecture the lovely simplicity of the Georgian homes in Britain and the United States was superseded by a hodge-podge of styles which reached a peak of ugliness in the so-called "early General Grant" architecture in the United States and in the late Victorian homes in England. The eloquent efforts by John Ruskin to bring about a revival of the Gothic produced little more than a series of architectural monstrosities. Perhaps the least unsuccessful structures of this period were the more or less exact copies of Classical and Gothic buildings. Included in this category are some of the best examples of collegiate Gothic and many of our public buildings which were copies of Roman Imperial styles. The nonfunctional character of most of these structures, however, has become increasingly apparent and many of them are now being replaced by less flamboyant but more practical buildings.

Since the end of World War I, however, a significant change has taken place in western architecture. This change has been brought out chiefly by a new set of conditions in the building industry. On the one hand, the spectacular rise in labor costs has caused the disappearance of hand craftsmanship and has created the necessity of adopting architectural designs of the utmost simplicity and functional character. On the other hand, a host of new materials and more efficient construction techniques have been introduced which have made possible the creation of new architectural styles within the limits of economic cost. As a result, western architecture is now displaying great vitality and adaptability to changing conditions. Perhaps this has been because architecture, under the pressure of economic circumstance, has become more of an engineering technique than a genuine art. There is no possibility today of developing a great new architectural style comparable to those of the past, all of which depended upon abundant supplies of cheap labor. Nevertheless, I can see no signs of decadence in contemporary western architecture.

With regard to painting Spengler's condemnation of the French Impressionists is based almost solely upon the lack of any spiritual content in their painting. He regarded this development as a fleeting product of Megalopolitan civilization and a breakdown of the great tradition of western art. In the triumph of the "plein-air" painting of the French school over the Rembrandt-brown he saw one more case of the hopeless resistance by soul against intellect and culture against civilization.

It is not difficult to agree with Spengler that 19th century Impressionism was a fleeting product of the civilized mind from which all spiritual content had disappeared. One must disagree, however, with his contention that French Impressionism was not great art because of the absence of spirituality. Certainly the painting of light by the French Impressionists was strictly within the Faustian tradition of depth perspective. Spengler not only agrees with this idea but even goes so far as to treat Impressionism in its generic meaning as a basic symbol of our Western Culture—not only in the arts but also in mathematics and physics. He merely insists that 19th Century Impressionism in painting had ceased to be great art because of the absence of any spiritual significance.

The Impressionist school was followed around the turn of the century by that of the so-called post-Impressionists, which included such great names as Van Gogh, Cezanne, Matisse, and Gauguin. By their non-realistic use of colors and by their treatment of forms and perspective these painters came close to the threshold of abstract art. From this point it was but a short step to cubism, futurism, surrealism, expressionism and all the other cults of modern abstract art.

It is evident that Western sculpture of the past century has passed through the same general phases as painting. Thus Auguste Rodin, one of the greatest sculptors since the Renaissance, must be classified as an Impressionist. Concurrently with painting, since the early years of the present century, sculpture has turned progressively in the direction of abstract representation. Everything that can be said about modern painting, therefore, applies with equal validity to contemporary sculpture.

Instead of condemning abstract art, in the manner of Spengler, as "impotence and falsehood," it is important to attempt to understand it. Above all, it represents a conscious revolt against the great traditions of our Faustian Culture. The 20th Century painter feels driven to seek new methods of expression, either because he realizes that he cannot hope to improve on the work of the great masters of the past, or because he has become satiated to the point of loathing with all previous efforts to portray realistic likenesses of human beings and their surroundings. The result has been a withdrawal into himself in an effort to express his own esthetic interpretation of life without the encumbrance of seeking to reproduce what the human eye usually sees in the external world. It seems clear that the perfecting of modern photography has played an important part in this trend. Thus, the modern painter cannot hope to compete with the realism of a colored photograph. His recourse, therefore, has been to move into the realm of abstraction. This whole development has been well described as "the dehumanization of art."[59]

While one must agree that there is much genuine sincerity and some beauty in modern abstract art, it does appear evident that this art form, with its highly subjective and esoteric approach, and its strong sense of irony, lends itself to various forms of charlatanism. For example, it is my opinion that much of the work of Salvador Dali falls in this category. Even some of the creations of Picasso, by his own admission, were done with his tongue in his cheek in an effort to produce a maximum of shocking power.

Probably the most important contribution of abstract art has been in the area of pure design. Here the complete freedom of the artist in combining a great variety of colors and lines has resulted in the production of many interesting and decorative patterns which are usually devoid of any symbolic meaning.

This brings us to the ultimate problem of the great bulk of contemporary art. The difficulty is that it has become in large measure the outward expression of a spiritual void within the artist himself—whether he be a painter, a sculptor, a poet or a musician. This predicament has been brought out vividly by a contemporary philosopher, William Barrett, in the following passage:—

"The modern artist sees man not as a rational animal, in the sense handed down to the West by the Greeks, but as

---

[59] Jose Ortega y Gasset, *The Dehumanization of Art;* Princeton Univ. Press, 1948.

something else. . . . 'Our time,' said Max Scheler, 'is the first in which man has become thoroughly and completely problematic to himself'. Hence the themes that obsess both modern art and existential philosophy are the alienation and strangeness of man in his world, the contradictoriness, feebleness and contingency of human existence; the central and overwhelming reality of time for man who has lost his anchorage in the eternal. . . . There is a painful irony in the new image of man that is emerging, however fragmentarily, from the art of our time. . . . The disparity between the enormous power which our age has concentrated in its external life, and the inner feebleness which our art seeks to expose to view."[60]

It is important here to distinguish between the absence of spiritual content in the art of the 19th century Impressionists and what is described above as the spiritual void in the typical abstract artist of today. On the one hand, the Impressionists displayed a kind of spiritual neutrality, or freedom from religious compulsion, while retaining a vivid sense of beauty and an exuberant vitality. In current abstract art, on the other hand, there is much evidence of a state of mind that must be characterized as a form of nihilistic despair which the artist himself can tolerate only by treating life as something of a cosmic joke.

I must conclude, therefore, that a high proportion of contemporary abstract art has ceased to be art in any proper meaning of the word. Nevertheless, one should recognize that the efforts of the 20th century artist to explore and experiment with new art forms are also part of the Faustian

---

[60]From THE IRRATIONAL MAN by William Barrett, copyright © 1958 by William Barrett. Reprinted by permission of Doubleday & Company, Inc.

tradition. He has been striving to break free from the old moulds and to create something fresh and vital. It is conceivable that he may succeed eventually in this endeavor but it is difficult to visualize such a development unless the artist can find a philosophy of life more inspiring than that of an alienated existentialist.

In the field of music, Spengler was clearly correct in asserting that the work of Wagner marked a decisive turning point in the evolution of this art. Certainly the great Baroque music of counterpart had passed its zenith and was beginning to break up into a variety of schools, such as the tone-poems introduced by Richard Strauss, and the Impressionistic school which appeared in France under the leadership of Debussy and Ravel. Nevertheless, while these developments may not be in the great tradition of Bach, Mozart and Beethoven, much of this later music has a strong and lasting appeal. Thus, the best of tone poems of Richard Strauss display a stirring vitality and much thematic beauty. Moreover, the music of the Impressionistic composers, such as that of Debussy and Ravel, must be accorded a significant place in the evolution of the art. In its effort to catch the mood of a fleeting moment it bears a close relationship to the Impressionistic phase of painting and sculpture, and has an equally strong sensuous appeal.

In the music of the 20th century, two separate and distinct trends should be noted. In popular music, particularly dance music, we have witnessed a return to primitivism in the form of modern "Jazz" and its more recent successors. Such dance music has become more and more an expression of primitive and uninhibited sex. The most popular dance orchestra of today is that which has the most strident beat and which also produces the greatest volume of sound.

Serious music, on the other hand, has continued the trend toward abstraction with increasing emphasis upon the use of minor keys and of deliberately introduced dissonances. There is one important factor in this trend that is usually ignored by the experts. This is the tendency on the part of the public to become satiated by any one type of music, and to demand something new and different. This propensity can be seen in connection with all art forms but is most noticeable in the case of music. Thus, even the magnificently rounded periods of the counterpoint of Mozart and Beethoven can have a cloying effect if heard too often. As a result, the public constantly feels the need for something stronger and harsher to satisfy its jaded ear. It is something like the need of a dope addict for stronger and stronger medicine in order to achieve the same effect. This tendency probably has been evident throughout history but has become increasingly apparent as a result of the rising tempo and growing tensions of modern life. It must have been an important factor in the great popularity of Wagner during his era, for the still harsher music of Richard Strauss and finally for the present-day appeal of Shostakovich and of other more recent composers. It is my opinion that such a trend can only be regarded as a sign of decadence.*

*No attempt is made in these pages to deal with the vast realm of Faustian literature. This omission is chiefly the result of the inadequacy of Spengler's treament of the subject. His discussion of literature is limited to a few broad and disjointed generalizations, such as the contrast between Classical and Faustian grand tragedy, and the biographical character of all Faustian literature. For a brilliant analysis of the decline of western drama, the reader's attention is directed to two essays by Joseph Wood Krutch with respective titles of *The*

Tragic Fallacy, and *Love—or the Life and Death of a Value*. These pieces are to be found in a collection of essays by Krutch published in 1929 by Harcourt, Brace & Co. with the title *The Modern Temper*.
It is also worth noting here that western poetry passed through a phase of Impressionism similar to that of the other great arts. This period lasted generally from about the middle of the 19th century through the first two decades of the present century. Thereafter, western poetry became increasingly abstract and esoteric, a trend which has continued up to the present day.

SOME FINAL OBSERVATIONS

The reader must now judge for himself whether or not all the evidence presented above does represent a decay of our western civilization. To my mind it seems clear that we are living today in a *Twilight of the Evening Lands*. Although the drift in this direction is not irreversible, this trend can be changed only if we recognize fully the dangers that threaten our society and, by a tremendous effort of the national will, restore a spirit of unity, order and self-discipline.

In this connection we should consider Spengler's general philosophy of life which may be of greater importance for the modern world than any of his specific predictions. It is a harsh doctrine and one that proved too strong for the stomachs of many of his contemporaries. It involves a belief in the need for a high sense of unity and discipline, and a strong militaristic spirit as the only means of survival in a chaotic world.

Can anyone seriously maintain that the passage of a half century has eliminated the need for such fundamental masculine virtues? Our present highly affluent and permissive society has reached a point where practically anything goes —pornography, sexual license, drug addiction, the beginning of a breakdown of law and order, and a threatened collapse of our educational system under the pressure of continuing revolts by white students and black militants.

Many, of course, will argue that a militaristic spirit has become an anachronism in a world armed with nuclear weapons. There is a vast difference, however, between an aggressive imperialistic militancy and a strong posture of military defense and a willingness to resist aggression. As pointed out earlier in this study, the age on military imperialism in the Faustian world came to an end during World War I, and has been succeeded by the rising imperialism of the Communist nations. Today we see nearly one-half of the world's population under Communistic domination, and the white races of the earth outnumbered by the colored by a three-to-one ratio. Under such circumstances, it should be obvious to all with a desire to understand that a continuing decay in our sense of unity and of our moral fiber, accompanied by a lowering of our military guard, can only invite the destruction of our western civilization. While we should continue to strive for peaceful coexistence with the Communist nations, we shall never achieve this goal by operating from a position of weakness. It is a hard world we live in, as it always has been, and the road to survival has never been found by those nations which permit themselves to become flabby as a result of too much affluence.

If, indeed, we are drifting down the road towards a police state, the question naturally arises as to the type of dictatorship that is most likely to emerge. Will it be a military dictatorship which would strive to maintain the existing social structure, or will it be a dictatorship modeled along communistic lines which would involve a destruction of the present social order? Unfortunately I do not possess a crystal ball to enable me to peer into the future and arrive at any such prediction, although I suspect that the latter eventuality is more likely than the former. The reason for this suspicion is that we in the United States do not possess the tradition of a strong hereditary aristocracy or a dominant church. It is these two factors which have been chiefly responsible for maintaining the military dictatorship in Spain but even there it is now becoming doubtful that the existing government can long survive the death of Franco. Finally, I cannot even venture a guess as to where, when and how a new high culture may appear on the face of the earth.

We have now reached the point of discussing the most fundamental of all questions for this study. What do we really mean by a decline of western civilization? Unless we are all wiped out by a nuclear holocaust, it certainly does not mean the disappearance of Western Man from the face of the earth. Nor does it mean the loss of all personal and human values. What it does mean is that we are living in an age of social revolution and of drastic changes in our accustomed patterns of existence. To many, particularly to members of the older generations, all violent changes are evidence of decay. For youth, however, such upheavals are often welcomed as exhilarating signs of progress. William Wordsworth, in his poem of reflections on the outbreak of the French Revolution, described this attitude of youth in the following lines:

> *"Bliss was it in that dawn to be alive,*
> *But to be young was very heaven!"*

The problem thus is largely one of adaptability, and the extent to which one is, or is not, frozen into a belief that a particular mode of life is the only one acceptable. Succeeding generations of mankind have proven themselves capable of an almost endless series of adaptations to new conditions of existence, and our children and grandchildren will be better able to cope with the changes that lie ahead than would be possible for the elderly adults who are alive today. Certainly many individuals found it possible to live satisfactory personal lives during the age of the Roman Empire, and there is reason to hope that the environment will not present greater difficulties during the civilization phase of our own Culture. As Spengler has pointed out, historical time is irreversible, and there is no psychological disease more damaging than an acute nostalgia for an irretrievable past.

No one, however, loves a prophet of gloom or doom, and the role is never a happy one to play. I discovered this truth for myself when I served as a professional business forecaster during the years 1929 through 1931. Thus, I learned that a forecaster who was consistently optimistic and wrong four times out of five was likely to be remembered for the one time he was right. On the other hand, a forecaster who was consistently pessimistic and right four times out of five would so anger his readers for being right that they would tend to remember only the time he was wrong. Because on this I abandoned the occupation.

We have come a long way since the early years of the 20th century when a belief in the steady amelioration of mankind had almost attained the status of a religious faith.

Under the impact of the events of the past half century this blind faith in unending human progress has largely disappeared. All educated individuals today are at least familiar with the idea of a decline of our civilization, even though they may not accept it as inevitable. It is chiefly for this reason that it is now possible to discuss Spengler's theories objectively and without stirring up the passions and prejudices which were so prevalent when the *Decline* first appeared.

Nevertheless, Western Man remains congenitally optimistic, and such an attitude is probably essential for his survival. If all of us despaired of the future, we would certainly lose our will to live, and there would cease to be a future. On the other hand, it is equally important that we become fully aware of the hard realities of the contemporary world and of the dangers which threaten our society. It is on this note that I bring this study to a close. I can think of no better way of doing so than by quoting the following lines of A. E. Housman which come close to expressing the essence of Spengler's philosophy, as well as my own:

> *"Therefore, since the world has still*
> *Much good, but much less good than ill,*
> *And, while the sun and moon endure*
> *Luck's a chance, but trouble's sure,*
> *I'd face it as a wise man would,*
> *And train for ill and not for good."*[61]

---

[61]From "Terence, this is stupid stuff:" from "A Shropshire Lad"—Authorized Edition—from THE COLLECTED POEMS OF A. E. HOUSMAN. Copyright 1939, 1940, © 1959 by Holt, Rinehart and Winston, Inc. Copyright © 1967, 1968 by Robert E. Symons. Reprinted by permission of Holt, Rinehart and Winston, Inc.

APPENDIX

Origins and Rationale of
Twentieth Century Liberalism

One of Spengler's important, but little noted contributions, is his contrast between the dominant philosophies of the Classical and Faustian civilizations. For Classical man in his civilization stage it was stoicism—a calm and static acceptance of the vicissitudes of life. For Faustian man, however, the more dynamic theory of socialism has become the dominant philosophy. Spengler defines socialism more broadly than a mere belief in any particular political faith, or a philosophy of human welfare. Instead, he describes it as an expression of the modern idea of *Progress* and the Faustian will-to-power. He states that the stoic takes the world as he finds it, but the socialist wants to recast it in form and substance, to fill it with his own spirit.

Modern socialism has its roots in the optimistic theory that all human problems can be solved by the application of human reason. Francis Bacon was a protagonist of this doctrine during the dawn of the modern age. He was followed in the eighteenth century by Rousseau and then by the philosophers of the French Revolution who even crowned a *Goddess of Reason*. From this time until the middle of the nineteenth century reason appeared to dictate a policy of *laissez-faire* because of the belief that the main problem was that of removing the shackles of government regulations from individual initiative, and that then the *invisible hand* of Adam Smith would lead humanity to unending progress.

Karl Marx, however, turned the trend away from *laissez-faire*. Although he preached revolution Marx remained essentially an optimist in his faith in the perfectibility of the human race and the anticipated withering away of government after the revolution. Nietzsche, of course, followed the same trend in his doctrine of the

Übermensch. Thus one can see clearly why Spengler described Nietzsche as a socialist.

During the past century the so-called liberal philosophy has abandoned completely the doctrine of *laissez-faire* and has moved progressively in the direction of imposed controls by government. This development, in its instinctive and compulsive efforts to remold modern man, brings the contemporary intellectual liberal very close to Spengler's definition of a socialist. The liberal philosophy, therefore, has become a prime expression of the Faustian will-to-power. Our liberals, of course, have maintained their faith in the steady amelioration of humanity and in the belief that all human problems can be solved by reason and by more and more egalitarianism. As such, they have become the outstanding optimists of the western world. The final tragedy for their doctrine, however, lies in the fact that the more the liberals succeed in their efforts the closer they bring us to a police state, in which most of the genuine liberals would be among the first to be liquidated.

Bibliography

BY SPENGLER

The Decline of the West; Vol. I: *Form and Actuality;* Vol. II: *Perspectives of World-History;* (Knopf, New York, 1926 and 1928)
Man and Technics: A Contribution to a Philosophy of Life (Knopf, New York, 1932)
The Hour of Decision: Part One: Germany and World-Historical Evolution (Knopf, New York, 1934)
Politische Schriften (Political Writings) (Munich, 1932)
Reden und Aufsätze (Speeches and Essays) (Munich, 1937)
Urfragen (Fundamental Questions) (Munich, 1965)
Frühzeit der Welt-Geschichte (Early Period of World History) (Munich, 1966)

ABOUT SPENGLER

Manfred Schröter, *Der Streit um Spengler* (The Spengler Controversy) (Munich, 1922) and *Metaphysik des Untergangs,* (Metaphysics of the Decline) (Munich, 1949)
Eduard Meyer, *Spenglers Untergang des Abendlandes* (Berlin, 1925)
André Fauconnet, *Un Philosophe Allemand Contemporain: Oswald Spengler;* (A Contemporary German Philosophy) (Paris, 1925)
E. H. Goddard and P. A. Gibbons, *Civilization or Civilizations: An Essay on the Spenglerian Philosophy of History,* (Boni and Liveright, New York, 1926)

R. G. Collingwood, *Oswald Spengler and the Theory of Historical Cycles;* (Antiquity: A Quarterly Review of Archaeology, September, 1927)

Arthur Mendel, *Spengler's Quarrel with the Methods of Music History;* (The Music Quarterly, April, 1934)

Edwin Dakin, *Today and Destiny:* (Knopf, New York, 1940)

Pitrim A. Sorokin, *Social Philosophies of an Age of Crisis;* (Beacon Press, Boston, 1950—Second Edition by Dover Publications, New York, 1963 with the title *Modern Historical and Social Philosophies*)

H. Stuart Hughes, *Oswald Spengler; A Critical Estimate;* (Scribners, New York, 1952—Revised Edition, 1962)

Spengler Studien; (A series of essays on Spengler written in commemoration of Manfred Schröter's 85th birthday) (Munich, 1965)

Bruce Mazlish, *The Riddle of History; The Great Speculators from Vico to Freud;* (Harper and Row, New York, 1966)

Anton Koktanek, *Oswald Spengler in Seiner Zeit;* (A comprehensive biography of Spengler), (Munich, 1968)

Index